A Welfare Mother

Susan Sheehan

With an Introduction
by Michael Harrington

HOUGHTON MIFFLIN COMPANY BOSTON · 1976

Most of the contents of this book originally appeared, in slightly different form, in *The New Yorker*. The Introduction by Michael Harrington is adapted from an article that originally appeared in [*MORE*]. The Afterword by Susan Sheehan is published here for the first time.

Library of Congress Cataloging in Publication Data
Sheehan, Susan. A welfare mother.
1. Santana, Carmen, 1932–   2. Welfare recip-
ients—New York (City)—Biography. 3. Puerto Ricans
in New York (City) I. Title.
HV99.N59S47   362.5'092'6   76-13439
ISBN 0-395-24505-2
Printed in the United States of America

V 10 9 8 7 6 5 4 3 2 1

For my mother and father

Introduction *by Michael Harrington*

Poverty is winning the social war and that is why this book is so important, for one reaction to that fact could be a tendency for the poor in America to become invisible once again.

This trend is already very much in existence. Not only traditional conservatives, like President Ford and Ronald Reagan, but one-time liberals, like Governers Brown of California and Dukakis of Massachusetts, are telling the nation that it tried too much in the sixties, that it must, therefore, now cut back. That issue is a complex one, but I think Daniel Patrick Moynihan summed up the facts accurately in his *Politics of the Guaranteed Annual Income,* a book that, since it makes Richard Nixon a hero, can hardly be accused of leftist bias. The social programs of the sixties, Moynihan wrote, were "oversold and underfinanced to the degree that their seeming failure was almost a matter of design." That is true, but it is a complicated truth, and a good many people are ready to accept the cruel simplification that we should stop doing so much for the poor.

The statistics on poverty are themselves depressing enough, but perhaps even more depressing is the fact that our entire welfare system, though it springs from generous motives, is somehow missing the whole point of the problem. Mrs. Santana, the protagonist of this book, is not really "poor" in the sense that she has no money to buy basic food and shelter; she is, rather, simply unable to cope with the demands and complications of life in present-day America. Her confrontations with the Welfare Department are not bitter or dishonest, but incomprehensible — or at least baffling — to both parties. Until the government bureaucracy can somehow be refocused or sensitized to the plight of people like Mrs. Santana, there is little hope that public welfare can ever accomplish more than an unsatisfactory way of continuing a hapless and hopeless group of recipients who will never become integrated into our society.

If that mood grows, the country will once again forget the poor. It is, after all, difficult to be inhumane to people when you look into their faces. But if they can be safely segregated in urban slums and Appalachian hollows, then they can be ignored. Instead of being callous, which goes against the truly generous grain of the American people, one can just be carefully amnesiac. So it is that, after all the governmental and media attention of the sixties, it is quite possible that the poor will simultaneously grow in numbers and lose in visibility. That is why Susan Sheehan's intimate portrait of Mrs. Santana, a welfare mother, comes at just the right moment.

This book grew out of a *New Yorker* article. That sounds a hopeful personal echo for me. *The New Yorker,* for all of its ads directed to the affluent, has long been an important source of social journalism in the United States. It printed John Hersey on Hiroshima and Rachel Carson on pesticides, and both authors had enormous impact. And its concern for poverty is not new, as I can attest from personal experience. My book, *The Other America,* appeared in March of 1962 to favorable, but not rave, reviews. By January 1963 I was in Paris working on *The Accidental Century* and I assumed that *The Other America* had run its course. In that month, *The New Yorker* printed Dwight Macdonald's long review — it was really an article on poverty organized primarily, but not exclusively, around a discussion of my book — and it had the effect of a second publication date. It was that event, and *The New Yorker,* that really made the study a matter for discussion in the northeast corridor. And, as far as I can figure out, it was in response to the renewed interest generated by the Macdonald review that John F. Kennedy borrowed a copy of *The Other America* from Walter Heller, read some other analyses, and decided to launch his attack on poverty.

However, what strikes me as particularly important — and new — about Susan Sheehan's work in *The New Yorker,* and now in this book, is that its center is not an analysis of poverty by a middle-class intellectual, but is a poor person presented in some depth. That, I think, is an extremely impor-

tant innovation. It communicates the human and particular
anguish of poverty, and even its occasional gaiety, and not
just the abstract numbers. It might force us to see.

Moreover, this portrayal of Mrs. Santana is just what the
middle-class people suspicious of welfare should read. In
the myth, the poor are sly, conniving cheats, parasitically living at the expense of the society, and living well. The welfare mothers, in particular, are seen as having babies just to
bid up their welfare checks. Mrs. Santana, the article makes
quite clear, does cheat, and so do most of her friends on welfare. But it is a cheating that arises out of necessity — the
checks just don't cover the basic needs of a family in New
York — and, most often, out of sexuality. The most common form of breaking the rules, which Mrs. Santana indulges
in, is to live with a man who makes money that is not reported to welfare. The actual income of the family is thus
considerably greater than the official payment.

Even so, this meticulous and undramatic account of Mrs.
Santana's day does not in the least communicate the picture
of a woman playing the system for all she can get. Mrs. Santana is clearly a victim, not a victimizer, and if she scrapes
some illegal dollars out of welfare, the cockroaches are still
crawling on the bread on the table, and a baby is found playing in dirty water on the floor. One of Mrs. Santana's children dropped out of school at fifteen and became a heroin addict; a daughter became pregnant when she was thirteen; and
another son, who has already failed a year of school, is about
to become a dropout. This is hardly the tale of a family
shrewdly using the society.

That point emerges in the depiction of family and sexual
life, too. Mrs. Santana's caseworker wants to know why she

had nine children. "He had been sure she had not had them simply to get more welfare," the author reports.

Anyone who had spent five years as a caseworker, as he had, knew that life for Puerto Rican women like Mrs. Santana was far more a series of accidents, both happy and unhappy, than popular wisdom realized. It was not in Mrs. Santana's nature to think about what she was going to eat for dinner until an hour or so before dinnertime, and it was not in her nature to go to bed with a man thinking that it might lead to an increase in her welfare check.

That is well said; moreover, it conforms to the results of some sophisticated research on welfare mothers. As Christopher Jencks reported in *Working Papers* some time ago, the data simply do not support the widespread belief that the large families of the poor are the result of calculation. Would that they were! Then one could solve the problem merely by raising the benefits to an adequate level, or by reducing the increments for an additional child at a certain point. Only it is not that easy. It is Mrs. Santana's culture, her way of life, not her monetary duplicity, that led to those nine children. She tried the pill but was frightened when her period stopped; and she has children born during the time that she was trying to use a diaphragm. The "serial monogamy" one discerns in Mrs. Santana's action is common in *all* poverty cultures in America; it is not Hispanic or black in origin.

Moreover, the crucial moment in Mrs. Santana's story is not a crafty flight from responsibility into welfare chiseling, but a series of fateful events that changed the life of a person trying very hard to make ends meet. In 1961, Mrs. Santana had been working at assembling handbags for forty-three dollars a week for some four and a half years. Her companion of that period, Mr. Santana, earned forty dollars a week running a leather-cutting machine. Thus, the combined income of two adult workers was just a bit over two dollars an hour! Then Mrs. Santana had to quit because of a pregnancy, and Mr. Santana was laid off. When she had had the baby, Mrs. Santana could not find an inexpensive babysitting replacement for her mother-in-law, who had gone back to Puerto Rico. At that point she went to welfare because there was no other way out.

When welfare worked out a budget in 1961, one of the incredible insanities of the social policy of the period came into play. The department figured out the total need for the family on a very modest semimonthly basis — the total for five people came to one hundred eight dollars and ten cents — but subtracted Mr. Santana's earnings, with welfare paying only the difference, or twenty dollars and forty-four cents. That amounted to a 100 percent tax on Mr. Santana's earnings, and hardly motivated him to get, or keep, a job. There have been some changes since then, and even Richard Nixon, with his Family Assistance Plan, wanted to reform this spectacularly counterproductive aspect of the system. The point is, practices like this made cheating a matter of survival; so did the unconscionably low pay in the economic underworld in which the Santanas worked.

Another important point: Susan Sheehan found that the welfare workers were, on the whole, warm and sympathetic in dealing with the Santana family. They seemed to respond to the kids, she reports; they were really concerned. This is important to state, since there is a popular — middle-class, liberal, and even radical — mythology that all welfare workers are cold, bureaucratic, and totally unfeeling. That is simply not the case. Such people are to be found, of course, but they are not the rule and, in any case, the administrators of the welfare system are almost as trapped and maimed by its inadequacies as those they help.

Finally, a word about the writing of Susan Sheehan's book, which raises some questions about "advocacy journalism" in general. The form is straight reportage with some direct quotations, but not too many. It is, then, quite unlike Oscar Lewis's brilliant editing of his tapes. The prose is spare and direct in the mode of the American realism of the thirties and the matter-of-fact style of *The New Yorker* in many of its pieces. This strategy works marvelously well. Mrs. Sheehan hardly ever steps out of the persona of the reporter; she is a camera's eye. And yet, her subject matter speaks volumes for itself, and without a single word of editorializing she communicates a basic message, one that *New Yorker* readers — and not they alone — desperately need. I am certainly not against advocacy journalism — my own work does not make the least pretense to neutrality — but I am profoundly impressed in this case by the tactic of letting the lives of the poor preach the sermon.

In the "Afterword," Susan Sheehan does give the reader a brief, fascinating glimpse into the writer's particular problems in dealing with this area of American life. It took her three months to find Mrs. Santana, because people who are on welfare are, of necessity, suspicious of every outsider. That is one mark of their alienation from the larger society. And it should be noted that not many journalists would have the patience, and then the courage, to break through that barrier, which is guarded by junkies in tenement hallways as well as by the psychological attitudes of the poor. But once on the other side of that chasm, which separates the other America from the rest of us, once some measure of trust was won, there was time for talk and even friendship.

We need to be reminded of these poignant and terrible things, of the bad and, yes, of the good within the culture of poverty. We are, I fear, preparing as a nation to turn our backs on suffering once again. But we have not made that immoral decision yet. So perhaps this compassionate book by Susan Sheehan can keep our eyes open. And if we see these things, would we have the perverse courage to turn away from them? I hope not. I even think not, which is why I am so enthusiastic about *A Welfare Mother*.

New York City
February 1976

A Welfare Mother

CARMEN SANTANA is a welfare mother. She lives in a four-room apartment in the Williamsburg section of Brooklyn with the four children she had by a man named Vicente Santana, whom she lived with from 1959, when she first came to New York City from Puerto Rico, until 1969. A present member of the household is Francisco Delgado, whom she took up with some months before she and Mr. Santana parted. Mr. Delgado is a quiet, good-looking, slender man of thirty-seven who wears a mustache. Mrs. Santana is a jolly, outgoing, notably stout woman of forty-three, and she approaches life with gusto. When she sees the villain in her favorite Spanish television soap opera behaving in a dastardly fashion, she jumps to her feet and moves close to the TV set, shaking her fist at him and cursing him roundly for a pimp and a thief. (Though she speaks adequate English, she speaks Spanish to her family and friends and curses in Spanish.) With equal gusto, when her children happen to displease her she gives them a good cuffing, and when — perhaps five minutes later — they happen to please her she gathers them in against her immense bosom and gives them a good hug. Mr. Delgado observes with admiration the changeable weather of Mrs. Santana's warm heart. He and she evidently enjoy each other's company; when they are seated on a sofa or on adjacent chairs, his arm finds its way around her broad back, and their conversation is merry and salacious.

Mrs. Santana's days are a round of small domestic melodramas, and she would not have it otherwise. She has no interest in national or international events; over the years, Vietnam, the Arab-Israeli wars, and the energy crisis have assuredly had an indirect effect on her, but she remains largely unaware of them. To an outsider, her world might seem very narrow; to her, it is ample. She faces every day with equanimity, hoping that something pleasant will befall her in the course of it, shrugging off her disappointment when it does not. What will be will be, whether good or bad. When she can afford to buy pork chops for dinner she buys pork chops, and when she cannot afford them she buys rice and beans. She makes little real effort to dominate circumstances; though she likes to draw up plans and gives every appearance of intending to carry them out, they are soon forgotten. She is at ease with time, which is to say that

she pays as little attention to it as possible. She is every bit
as vague about days as her children are; nobody in the family
troubles to remember the year in which he was born, and
when someone says "next week" he may well mean "next
month." Whenever Mrs. Santana has to wait in line for
something, she is contentedly resigned; it would never occur
to her to turn the time to her advantage by reading or sewing.

Mrs. Santana loves to dance; otherwise, she avoids all
physical exercise. She sits even while she is cooking, and
she would rather leave the TV on when she isn't watching it
than bother to get up and turn it off. Her obesity appears to
cause her no distress — she likes the way she looks and so
does Mr. Delgado. ("It's as easy to make love to a fat
woman as a skinny one.") She makes no effort to conceal
her thick neck, her big breasts, her big belly, and her enormous thighs; on the contrary, she favors tight-fitting, scoop-
necked body shirts with Bermuda shorts or slacks. Because
of her weight, she is unable to take off her fashionable platform shoes unaided. Dancing, she quickly loses breath, but
she goes on dancing. She is generous and lazy. Nothing
lasts long in her apartment; it passes from being brand-new to
being either broken or lost or stolen or given away.

The apartment, which Mrs. Santana and Mr. Delgado
moved into four years ago, is on the second floor of a four-
story walkup building that has seen better days. It consists
of a small living room, two small bedrooms, a small
bathroom (which has a tub and a toilet but no washbasin),
and a good-sized kitchen. The bedroom that Mrs. Santana
and Delgado share contains a double bed; a dresser cluttered
with a multitude of lipsticks, perfumes, hair sprays, and other
cosmetics; a black and white television set; a small table cov-

ered with china figures; and a telephone — the first telephone Mrs. Santana has ever had. The room has no closet, and Mrs. Santana's clothes hang on pegs driven into the bright pink walls. Until a few weeks ago, all of Delgado's clothes hung on the pegs, too. On a recent Saturday afternoon, he gathered up his clothes and went off to his sister's place, in Manhattan. He stayed away from the apartment that Saturday night for no apparent reason: he had not been drinking that day, and there had been no quarrel on Friday. He returned on Sunday evening with no explanation and with only a few of his clothes, and has yet to bring the rest of his wardrobe back.

The second bedroom is furnished with nothing but a bunk bed and an infant's stroller. It is occupied by Vicente Santana, thirteen years old; Emilio Santana, twelve; Gabriel Santana, eleven; and María Santana, ten. The two older children sleep in the top bunk, the two younger ones in the lower. The children's clothes are piled up on the stroller. They have decorated their vivid yellow walls with graffiti, many of which are obscene, a few not. The living room is furnished with a green and gold couch, a green and gold armchair, an aqua and gold armchair, a coffee table, a lamp, a radio-phonograph, and a black and white television set. Although the couch and the armchairs are protected by plastic covers, and although Mrs. Santana bought the three pieces only a year and a half ago, they are in a sorry state. Vicente, Emilio, Gabriel, and María are hard on the furniture, and so are Mrs. Santana's grandchildren, who visit her often; they are the young sons and daughters of five children she had by two men in Puerto Rico before she came to New York. The kitchen contains a gas stove, an electric refrigerator, a sink,

an automatic washing machine, a cupboard, and a small For-
mica dinette table and four chairs. Its floor is covered with
peeling linoleum, as are all the other floors in the apartment.
Each room has a bare bulb on the ceiling, and a window.
The windows face an empty apartment building (a bad fire
gutted it several years ago) and a courtyard that is strewn
with refuse. Mrs. Santana and her children contribute to the
refuse by throwing their trash and garbage out their windows.
The apartment is not much different from ten other apartments Mrs. Santana has lived in, on the lower East Side of
Manhattan and in Brooklyn, over the past sixteen years.
Some were smaller — her first apartment, with Santana, had
only two rooms — and some were larger; once, when six of
her nine children were living with her, she had a six-room
apartment. All the apartments have had peeling paint, falling
plaster, rats, cockroaches, and unreliable heating and hot
water. They have all been in aging walkup buildings marred
by landlord violations and tenant abuses. "No apartment
I've had in New York has been as nice as the one I moved
into in Puerto Rico when I was fourteen and just married,"
Mrs. Santana says. "I lived in a project then. The floors
were so new they didn't have to be covered with anything. I
had two easy chairs, two rocking chairs, lamps, a sofa, a
table, and a radio in my living room, and a pretty bedroom
set. I had everything good."

Mrs. Santana (no actual names have been used in this
book) was born Carmen Casilda Ramírez, in Cayey, a small
town in south-central Puerto Rico, on September 2, 1932.

Her mother, Esperanza Ramírez, who lived in Cayey and worked as a maid, had gone to the nearby town of Cidra late in 1931 to visit some aunts. In Cidra, she met a bookkeeper named Julio Vásquez, became pregnant with his child, and returned to Cayey before she knew of her condition. Carmen was the second of three children Esperanza Ramírez was to have, by three different men, none of whom she married; she had a daughter four and a half years before Carmen was born and a son three and a half years after. Mrs. Santana doesn't know why her grandparents never forced her mother to marry any of the fathers of her children. Esperanza Ramírez died at the age of twenty-eight, while having an abortion; Carmen was five at the time, and she scarcely remembers her mother. Carmen's father wasn't told of her birth, and she was called Carmen Ramírez. When she was eleven, her father dreamed that Esperanza Ramírez was dead, went to Cayey, learned of his daughter's existence, and gave her his surname; thereafter she was Carmen Vásquez.

Carmen was born in the home of her maternal grandparents and was brought up by them. Her grandmother, Olga Ramírez, was of Indian descent and worked in a tobacco factory. Her grandfather, Raul Ramírez, a blue-eyed white man whose ancestors came from Spain, drove an oxcart until a wagon wheel ran over one of his feet and forced him to lead a sedentary life. Mrs. Santana recollects that her grandparents, both now dead, were legally married and had seven or eight children. She doesn't know where her grandparents were born, and she doesn't know anything at all about their parents — not even their names. Who her great-grandparents were has never been of any interest to her. Mrs. Santana takes after her grandmother. She has Olga Ramírez's dark eyes, wide nose, mulatto complexion, curly black hair, thick lips, broad face, and prominent cheekbones. When Mrs. Santana came to New York, sixteen years ago, she was a size 9. She gained a lot of weight during each of her last four pregnancies, and now weighs more than two hundred pounds and wears a size 20.

The house in which Carmen grew up, along with a few of her cousins, was a frame structure that lacked electricity, plumbing, and running water. One of her childhood chores was fetching water from the public pump. There was always enough to eat, but the family was poor, and Carmen went to school in rags, often without shoes. The only toy she was ever given was a five-cent balloon. Her grandparents were ardent Catholics; they saw to it that she made her First Communion, was confirmed, and attended Mass every Sunday. They were also very strict, rarely letting her out of the house. She was forbidden to see movies or to keep company with boys. Whenever she sneaked out of the house and was caught, she was beaten severely. "My childhood wasn't much fun," Mrs. Santana says, in a way that suggests that she hadn't expected it to be otherwise. Mrs. Santana worries a good deal about her four younger children; it is likely that they will soon start either using drugs or selling them, as two of their older brothers have already done. "In some ways, my children are having a better childhood than I had," she says. "They have nicer clothes, they have more things, and they have more liberty than I had, but Cayey was an easier place than New York for keeping out of trouble."

There was a garage between Carmen's home and her school. When she was fourteen and in the ninth grade, she became friendly with a mechanic who worked there, a twenty-four-year-old veteran of the Second World War named Rafael Rodríguez. He was going out with another girl when they met, but she stopped in to visit him at the garage often, and they fell in love. One Saturday, when she was out selling chances on a ring someone was raffling, she and Rafael Rodríguez eloped to his mother's house. He took her to bed. It was the first time she had made love to a man. "I didn't even know what he wanted me for," Mrs. Santana says, entertained some twenty-nine years later by the thought of her remembered innocence. "In my grandparents' house, there was no sex, only religion." The day after the elopement, Carmen's grandmother came, in tears, to get her at Rafael's mother's house, took her home, sent for her father (who was then living in Mayagüez), and locked her up for the three days it took him to get to Cayey. A daughter who was not a virgin was no longer readily marriageable. Her father quickly determined that Rafael Rodríguez was willing to marry her — if he had refused, he could have gone to jail for corrupting a minor — and signed the papers giving his consent to the marriage of a minor. The couple were married on October 20, 1946, in a civil ceremony, which had the advantage of taking less time to arrange than a religious ceremony; they were attended only by the bride's father and two witnesses. The bride wore a new flowered dress. There were no festivities. "We celebrated in bed," Mrs. Santana says. After her marriage, she stopped going to school, and she also stopped going to church regularly. She had once thought she would finish high school and become a nurse or a seamstress, but today she hardly remembers the plans she had when she was young. "I forgot school when I met Rafael Rodríguez," she says, without a trace of regret.

At the time of their marriage, Rodríguez was earning about ninety dollars a month as a mechanic. He was also getting a hundred and five dollars a month to study; as Mrs. Santana recalls it, this was some sort of veteran's benefit. She doesn't know where Rodríguez served during the war, or whether he did any fighting. She doesn't know what he was studying — only that he stopped studying after a while. At first, they lived with his widowed mother, who taught her how to cook. Shortly after their marriage, they moved into a new housing project for which veterans were eligible. The rent for the apartment, which Mrs. Santana recalls as the best place she has ever lived in, was only fourteen dollars a month. Her life with Rodríguez was pleasant. She cooked, cleaned, listened to soap operas on the radio, played dominoes with friends, and spent a lot of time hanging around the garage where her husband worked. In 1947, she gave birth — in the apartment — to a boy, who died of a urethral infection when he was three days old. On August 10, 1948, a few weeks before her sixteenth birthday, she bore — also in the apartment — a healthy thirteen-pound daughter, whom she named Casilda. Shortly after Casilda's birth, Rodríguez decided to go to the United States to work. His young wife was surprised at his decision and opposed it; their first two years had been good ones, and she believed he was earning enough money in Puerto Rico without having to go elsewhere to earn more. Rodríguez left for New York anyway. His wife heard, via the grapevine, that Rodríguez liked to fool around with women in New York, but he sent her money fairly regularly and returned periodically to Puerto Rico. On November 10, 1950, nine months after one of her husband's visits, Rafael Rodríguez, Jr., was born. Carmen

Rodríguez had moved back to her grandmother's house after her husband left for the United States; later, she moved to an aunt's house. While one or another of her relatives watched the children, she did washing and ironing and housework to supplement the money Rodríguez sent, which lessened as time went by. On another of Rodríguez's visits, she became pregnant again. Rodríguez returned to New York in July of 1953, a month before his son Felipe Rodríguez was born, and didn't return to Puerto Rico again for many years. In New York, he had encountered the woman he had been seeing in Puerto Rico before his marriage, and he was living with her. "Rafael Rodríguez was a good man," Mrs. Santana says. "We didn't fight. He came here to America and found another woman and forgot me with three children in Puerto Rico. At first, I couldn't believe it. When we married, I thought the marriage would last forever."

During Rodríguez's absences from Puerto Rico, Carmen Rodríguez had started seeing seventeen-year-old Angel Castillo. One of her daughter Casilda's earliest memories is of Castillo clambering out the window of their house. In early 1955, Carmen Rodríguez, then twenty-two, began living with Castillo, who was a field worker on his family's farm. Neither she nor Castillo earned much money, so her two older children lived with Rodríguez's mother. In 1955, Rodríguez, who had moved from New York to Detroit, sent for Casilda and Rafael, Jr., and they went to live with him. In 1957, he wanted to marry the woman he was living with, and he wrote and asked his wife for a divorce, to which she consented. Although Carmen Rodríguez never married Castillo, she refers to him as her second husband — "husband" is a term she uses for any man she is living with, whether in or out of wedlock — and they had two daughters: Hilda, in August of 1956, and Inocencia, in February of 1958. From the start, Angel Castillo's mother took a dark view of her son's attachment. Carmen was older than her son and had already had children. She questioned Carmen's morals, and when Hilda was born, Castillo's mother went around saying Hilda was not his child. Shortly before Hilda's birth, Castillo got a thirteen-year-old girl pregnant. Castillo's mother forced her son to marry the girl, but he continued living with Carmen after his marriage. Not long after the birth of her daughter Inocencia, Carmen decided to leave Castillo, because she had had enough of his mother's nasty tongue. Castillo never earned much money, and he constantly played around with other women during their three years together, but Mrs. Santana always refers to him as her favorite husband. "He was a very handsome man, he was romantic, he really loved me," she says.

CARMEN RODRÍGUEZ's younger brother, Jaime Ramírez, who had been raised by his paternal grandmother, had moved to New York in the mid-fifties. Early in 1959, he sent Carmen a one-way plane ticket from San Juan to New York. At the time, she was working six days a week to earn nine dollars as a cook in a restaurant in Cayey. She had heard that salaries in New York were higher. To hear some people tell it, she says, there was gold lying about on the streets of New York. She flew to New York in April of 1959 with fourteen-month-old Inocencia. She intended to send for Felipe Rodríguez, whom she had left with Rodríguez's mother, and for Hilda Castillo, who had stayed with Castillo's mother, as soon as she was properly settled. Felipe did join her in 1960, but Castillo refused to send Hilda to New York. At nineteen, Hilda still lives in Puerto Rico with her grandmother. She is the only one of Mrs. Santana's children who has never even visited the United States.

For several months after arriving in New York, Carmen and Inocencia stayed with Jaime Ramírez and his wife, Mercedes, in their apartment on the lower East Side. Mercedes Ramírez took out on Carmen the resentment she felt toward her husband, who was having an affair with another woman. She refused to take care of the baby when Carmen wanted to go job-hunting, and she begrudged her her food. While Jaime Ramírez was at his factory job or dallying with his latest girl friend, Mercedes Ramírez preferred having some fun for herself to baby-sitting or cooking. After several months, Carmen and her baby moved a few blocks away, to the apartment of one of her maternal aunts. In September of 1959, she found a job at a leather-goods factory on lower Broadway and a new "husband," Vicente Santana. He had come to New York in April from his home in Caguas, was living with relatives in her aunt's building, and had also found work in a leather-goods factory. He was twenty-five — two years younger than Carmen — and had a wife and three children in his home town. He and Carmen started living together, first in a two-room apartment, then in a three-room apartment on the lower East Side, which they furnished with a few shabby beds, chairs, and odds and ends they had found on the street. Looking back to the start of what was to prove a tempestuous ten-year liaison, Mrs. Santana admits that she cared for Santana at the outset. This strikes her as ridiculous

now; no matter — her first feelings about him were irrele-
vant. "I needed a man then for money, not for love," she
says. "I couldn't support myself and two children."

During their first year and a half together, Santana earned
forty dollars a week operating leather-cutting machines, and
Mrs. Santana earned forty-three dollars a week assembling
handbags — a job she liked reasonably well. Santana's
mother lived nearby, with one of her daughters, and charged
Carmen ten dollars a week for baby-sitting for Felipe Rodríguez, Inocencia Castillo, and, eventually, for their first
child, Vicente Santana. Her next three children arrived in
rapid succession: Emilio fourteen months after Vicente, Gabriel fifteen months after Emilio, and María a year after Gabriel. When Mrs. Santana was pregnant with Emilio, her
mother-in-law returned to Puerto Rico for a visit. Mrs. Santana couldn't find an inexpensive baby sitter to replace her,
and so had to quit her job; a few months later, Santana was
laid off from his job for a week because it was a slow period
at the leather-goods company. Mrs. Santana had heard about
welfare from Santana's sister, and decided to apply for it.

A Department of Welfare employee took down the family's social history and economic situation. On a form called
a Family Budget Worksheet the employee recorded the
amounts of money the department calculated that two grownups and three children needed semimonthly for food, utilities,
and laundry; what they were paying for rent; and what Santana's work-related expenses were. The department then
added up the figures (they came to one hundred eight dollars
and thirty cents), subtracted Santana's semimonthly earnings
(eighty-seven dollars and sixty-six cents), and thus determined that the family's income was insufficient to meet its

needs. The Welfare Department opened only one case for the Santana household but sent two checks to cover the budget deficit of twenty dollars and forty-four cents. Santana and Vicente received a check for eight dollars and seventy-one cents under the department's Home Relief category. Mrs. Santana and her two children by other men received a check for eleven dollars and seventy-three cents in the Aid to Dependent Children category. It was the Department of Welfare that gave Mrs. Santana her official welfare surname. Although Puerto Rican women call the men they are living with their husbands even when they are living together without benefit of clergy, they don't use their surnames unless they marry them legally. Carmen Vásquez became Mrs. Rafael Rodríguez when she married, and kept that name until her divorce, when she became Carmen Vásquez once again. She has never remarried and has never called herself Mrs. Castillo, Mrs. Santana, or Mrs. Delgado, but to a Welfare Department employee in 1961 she was Vicente Santana's common-law wife, Mrs. Santana. Her welfare checks are still made out to Carmen Santana — a name none of her friends or relatives knows her by.

The first semimonthly Family Budget Worksheet drawn up for the Santanas by the Welfare Department in 1961 appears on the following page.

Over the next few years, Santana's paychecks gradually increased — by 1966, he was making sixty-five dollars a week in the leather-goods factory — but so did the number of children in the Santana household, the rent the family had to pay as they moved from one apartment to another (sometimes to get more space, sometimes because the building they were in was condemned, and once because their apartment

	Aid to Dependent Children	Home Relief
Individual allowance		
Mrs. Santana	16.75	
Felipe Rodríguez	13.35	
Inocencia Castillo	9.95	
Mr. Santana		17.75
Vicente Santana		9.95
Shelter [the monthly rental on their apartment was $40 and was split, 60–40, between A.D.C. and H.R., as were all other family expenses]	12.00	8.00
Utilities allowance	2.22	1.48
Laundry allowance [the family had no washing machine]	1.29	.86
Santana's work-related expenses — $9.25 for lunches, $3.25 for carfare, $2 for union dues		14.50
TOTAL	55.56	52.54
Santana's salary [every month except February has slightly more than four weeks; a $40-per-week salary is equal to 87.66 semimonthly]	− 43.83	− 43.83
DEFICIT	11.73	8.71

was destroyed by fire), and their other living costs. Since Santana was paid only for the days he actually worked, his income was smaller and the family's welfare payments were correspondingly larger when he stayed home — because of illness, or when the leather-goods factory closed for the Jewish holidays or for Christmas week or during a transit strike or during a slack period. Between 1961 and 1966, the semimonthly checks slowly increased from an average of about twenty dollars every two weeks to an average of about forty dollars every two weeks; they were much larger after 1968, when Santana stopped working altogether. Hardly any two consecutive checks the Santanas received were alike, because the Department of Welfare attempted to take every new development in the family's situation into account. When Gabriel was hospitalized for dehydration for a couple of months, shortly after his birth, his semimonthly food allowance of nine dollars and ninety-five cents and his fifty-nine-cent diaper-laundering allowance were deducted from the family's expenses for the duration of his hospital stay. When each of the children reached the approximate age of two, his or her laundry allowance was eliminated. When the Santanas occupied a particularly dark apartment, or one in which the heating system didn't function and they had to turn up the gas stove and move their mattresses to the kitchen to keep warm, they received an extra allowance for electricity or gas.

In addition to the semimonthly checks, the Santanas received periodic special grants, mostly for furniture and clothing, until 1968, when such grants were virtually stopped. A few weeks before Emilio was due, Mrs. Santana asked the Welfare Department to provide a homemaker to care for Felipe, Inocencia, and Vicente during the time she would be hospitalized. Before the department could assign one of its homemakers, an inventory of the apartment's contents had to be taken by the Santanas' caseworker and a Department of Welfare home economist. In their judgment, the Santanas' found-on-the-street furniture was inadequate, and they gave the family a grant of two hundred thirty-seven dollars for furniture to bring their three-room apartment "up to standard." The Santanas received other furniture grants when they moved to larger apartments, when all their possessions were destroyed by fire, and on numerous occasions when their caseworkers decided they were entitled to items that they lacked or that had worn out — a crib and a chest of drawers for a new baby, Mrs. Santana's first wringer washer ("She is an overburdened mother"), mattresses to replace those that had become soiled as a result of having been placed near kitchen stoves in unheated apartments. Over the years, the Santanas received quite a few beds, sofas, chairs, square yards of linoleum, window shades, curtains, towels, sheets, bedspreads, china place settings, pots and pans, mops and brooms, and an inordinate number of garbage pails and dishpans. The caseworkers rarely asked what had become of last year's garbage pail and dishpan, nor did they inquire how, on a welfare budget, the Santanas had acquired two television sets and a radio-phonograph. Clothing grants were usually given to the Santanas whenever their caseworker was told that the children couldn't attend school for lack of clothing or whenever Mrs. Santana presented the caseworker with a list of the new winter coats, spring coats, rain gear, shoes, overalls, sweaters, and the like that the various members of the family required. In addition to these furniture and clothing grants, the Department of Welfare periodically replaced cash or welfare checks that the Santanas reported had been lost or stolen: a check that was in a pocketbook Mrs. Santana left in the ladies' room at Bellevue Hospital's Prenatal Clinic in 1962; ninety dollars contained in a wallet that Santana dropped in a park in 1963 while he was playing baseball;

some cash that was in a purse that was snatched from Mrs. Santana after she left a bank on the lower East Side in 1969. The money taken from Mrs. Santana on that occasion was thirty-five dollars, but she claimed that the entire proceeds of her check — one hundred seventy dollars — had been stolen, because a friend had told her the department wouldn't replace small amounts. Mrs. Santana is a truthful woman except when truthfulness conflicts with her economic interests.

Mrs. Santana's case file from 1961 to the present consists of over seven hundred separate items. It includes letters from the Department of Welfare to Angel Castillo (whose address, in Puerto Rico, Mrs. Santana had supplied) asking him to support Inocencia, and his reply: he said he couldn't afford to support Inocencia, because he was supporting his daughter Hilda and several younger children. It also includes letters to Rafael Rodríguez's mother, in Puerto Rico, asking for her son's address, so that he could be asked to support Felipe. Mrs. Santana had said that she didn't know his whereabouts, and Mrs. Rodríguez claimed that she didn't know, either. There are statements signed by Santana acknowledging paternity of Vicente, Emilio, Gabriel, and María; reports on the children's schoolwork; the estimates from three different stores for wringer washers that Mrs. Santana was required to obtain before she was allowed to buy one; and numerous overdue-account notices and notices of disconnection of service from Con Edison. The Santanas often failed to pay their utility bills, and in 1963 the Department of Welfare "restricted" their utilities; that is, it paid the Santanas' Con Edison bills by making out two-party checks and took their utilities allowance off their budget. At the same time, the Welfare Department removed the rent allowance from their budget, too, and issued them two-party rent checks, which had to be endorsed by Santana and the landlord before they could be cashed.

In 1961, when the Santanas went on welfare, a caseworker from their local welfare center was assigned to them; this was the first of many caseworkers they had over the next ten years. It was her caseworker whom Mrs. Santana went to see whenever she needed something: a special grant, help in replacing a welfare check that had got lost in the mail, help with the paperwork involved in moving from one apartment to another. Part of the caseworker's job was to visit each client — in the sixties, the caseworker had anywhere from sixty to a hundred clients — at home at least four times a year. On these four statutory visits, the caseworker was supposed to review the clients' continued eligibility for welfare and to see how well they were managing. Every three months, the caseworker asked to look at Santana's paycheck stubs and the receipts showing that the Santanas' rent and utility bills had been paid; he also asked whether the family had any financial resources besides Santana's paychecks and their welfare checks. One caseworker after another took Mrs. Santana's word that these were her only resources ("Family advised no concealed resources," they duly recorded), although this was one matter on which Mrs. Santana's word was not always to be relied on. After Santana's mother returned from her visit to Puerto Rico, in December of 1961, and resumed baby-sitting for her, Mrs. Santana worked on and off in factories, without the Welfare Department's knowledge, until 1963. In the late sixties, she spent a good deal of her time on the street selling numbers, occasionally earning as much as a hundred dollars a day. She was arrested and taken to jail three times and was once fined fifty dollars, but the Department of Welfare never learned of her profitable illegal activities or of her arrest record.

The caseworkers were supposed to take notes on all their clients' visits to the welfare office and on all their own visits to the clients' homes — notes that were later typed up and inserted in the file. Between 1961 and 1971 (when caseworkers were no longer assigned to specific families, and regular home visits were stopped), a series of sixteen young men and women with Jewish, Italian, Irish, or Anglo-Saxon surnames called on the Santanas over periods ranging from a month to two years. Sometimes the Santanas got a new caseworker when they moved and their case was transferred to another local welfare center, but more often their caseworker left the Department of Welfare for another job. By far the most interesting pages in the Santanas' voluminous file are the caseworkers' notes, perhaps as much because of what they show about the Department of Welfare as because of what they show about the Santanas.

The notes indicate that the caseworkers were all fond of Mrs. Santana and of her children: the adjectives most frequently used to describe them are "warm" and "friendly." It is equally clear that the caseworkers were distressed by the family's living conditions and modus vivendi. Whereas some of the caseworkers simply described Mrs. Santana's dismal surroundings — the broken front doors and mailboxes, the overloaded electric sockets, the lopsided stoves with no oven doors, the rodents crawling in and out of holes, the dimly lit and grubby hallways, the cracked bathroom ceilings, the cockroaches and other insects, the

odors in the air, the shaky stairways that lacked banisters —
some of them also noted that "our client does not keep a
clean house" and that "the Santana children are rather de-
structive and there has been much damage done to the walls
and floors," and offered Mrs. Santana some housekeeping
hints. "We also pointed out to Mrs. Santana her need to
clean the stove and advised her how she could clean the
burners," wrote one caseworker with a penchant for referring
to himself in the first person plural. "The refrigerator, although in use at the present time, had not been washed, and
we suggested to the family that they wash the refrigerator
using baking soda or some other solvent cleaner."

If anything distressed the caseworkers more than Mrs. Santana's "very sloppy" housekeeping, it was her failure to get
her children to school regularly. In this area, too, the bak-
ing-soda proponents gave Mrs. Santana the benefit of their
advice. Here are four entries made by three caseworkers
over one nine-month period:

Worker visited Mrs. Santana's home and found the children
home alone . . . with exception of the baby [Gabriel]. Mrs.
Santana's son Felipe was preparing to scrub the floor. Felipe
who is nine years of age and very small for his age had this
big pail of water and had put in some soap detergent. We
questioned him as to . . . what he was planning to do and he
stated he was going to scrub the floor. We wondered why and
he stated he always scrubbed the floor. The children were all
playing in the water, even to the baby [Emilio]. We advised
Felipe that we wanted him to discard the water as we felt that
he was too young to have water without his mother's presence
in the home.

We questioned Felipe as to where his mother went and he
told us that she went to the hospital. He stated that he stayed
out of school to keep the children.

Worker visited Mrs. Díaz in apartment #5. We questioned Mrs. Díaz as to whether Mrs. Santana had inquired as to whether she would take care of the children and she told us that she had not. We inquired of Mrs. Díaz whether she would take care of the children until Mrs. Santana returned to the home. Mrs. Díaz stated she would.

[The same caseworker]: Mrs. Santana in the Welfare Center. She stated that she had to go to the hospital with the baby and she had no one to keep the children. We advised Mrs. Santana that we did not want the children left in the home alone as it was quite dangerous due to fires. She told us that she had done that quite often and she felt that there was no danger involved. We pointed out to Mrs. Santana very serious difficulties, and she stated that she would never leave the children home alone again. She told us that whenever she asked neighbors to keep the children they usually wanted pay. We wondered as to whether she ever did any favors for her neighbors and she stated she did. We suggested that they try and combine their little favors in order to protect the children.

[A new caseworker's first visit]: At the time of this visit, the apartment was very dirty and untidy. There were dirty dishes all over the kitchen and wet diapers and puddles of water on the floors. The beds were unmade. The worker discussed with Mrs. Santana the importance of keeping the apartment clean, particularly in a building which was known to have rats periodically. Mrs. Santana stated that she would try to keep the apartment in better condition in the future . . .

Client requested clothing for the entire family. At the time of our visit Emilio and Vicente were wearing no clothing, Gabriel was wearing a diaper, Inocencia was wearing a very torn dress and Felipe was wearing very dirty pants with large holes in them and a woolen shirt. Mrs. Santana explained that Felipe had stayed home from school as he didn't have clothing and that the children did not have better clothes to wear. Worker explained to her the importance of school attendance and she agreed to try to see that Felipe went to school every day.

[Another caseworker's first visit]: Felipe is in the fourth grade at PS 61. However, he had not been going to school because Mr. and Mrs. Santana said "he did not have shoes." They meant, though, that he did not have shoelaces. Worker suggested that they buy Felipe shoelaces immediately, and that this was no reason to stay out of school. Worker emphasized the importance of constant attendance in school. Inocencia, the five-year-old girl, has not started kindergarten yet because the school must receive her birth certificate from Puerto Rico. She should be going to kindergarten.

Mrs. Santana's stove is as grimy today as it was a decade ago, and her refrigerator does not look as if it had ever been subjected to a solvent cleaner. As for Felipe Rodríguez, in 1968, when he was fifteen and in the seventh grade, he dropped out of school and soon became addicted to heroin. Inocencia Castillo dropped out of the seventh grade in October of 1971, when she was thirteen and was three months pregnant with her first child. Vicente Santana is now in the seventh grade — he has failed a year — and may well drop out of school before the year is over.

WHEN caseworkers came to visit the Santanas during their first four years on welfare, Santana was almost always at work; he held the same job with the same leather-goods company from 1959 to 1966. If he happened to be at home during the caseworkers' visits in those early years, they found him "pleasant" but "not very communicative."

Whereas Mrs. Santana was willing to talk about her past, Santana was closemouthed about his. He "was unable to give us any information regarding his social history," one caseworker recorded. Another learned only that he had a tenth-grade education. He told a caseworker he was "satisfied" with his job at the factory, believed he was "working at capacity," and "would not be interested in rehabilitation of any kind." Mrs. Santana usually said that the family was "managing fairly well," but from a few remarks she made to her first caseworkers it was apparent that she didn't find Santana easy to live with. On being informed early in 1963 that the hours of the homemaker who was to take care of the older children while she was in the hospital having Emilio were 9:00 A.M. to 4:00 P.M., she warned the caseworker that Santana was "not responsible and returns home all sorts of time around eleven or twelve o'clock every night." Her warnings were later corroborated by the homemaker assigned to the family after María's birth. This homemaker, who stayed with the Santanas longer than her predecessors because Mrs. Santana had a tubal ligation after María was born and required additional bed rest, objected to "Mr. Santana's frequent lateness in returning home to relieve me." Mrs. Santana also complained about Santana's drinking and mentioned that she was thinking of leaving him. The caseworker counseled Mrs. Santana to visit her local church and ask for advice, and noted, "We further told her that it would be most beneficial to the children if Mr. and Mrs. Santana do not separate."

In August of 1966, Santana quit the job he had held for seven years. A caseworker visited the family a month later and wrote that Mr. Santana had quit "because the foreman, whose name is Johnny, did not like Mr. Santana and Mr. Santana was made to do heavy work, which he did not do due to his health.'' The caseworker instructed Santana to get a medical examination — he did, and was found healthy enough to do light work — and then to seek a job. On that visit, Santana also said that he and his wife weren't getting along and couldn't live together anymore. Several days later, Mrs. Santana called on her caseworker and said the same thing. In December of 1966, Santana got a job in another leather-goods factory, and for the next year the Santanas didn't discuss a possible separation with their caseworkers. Santana was fired from his job in December of 1967, after missing several weeks of work in November, because, so Santana told the caseworker, ''his boss believed he was lazy and did not want to work.'' Santana was right: when the caseworker queried his boss, the boss said he believed that Santana was ''lazy, unreliable, typical relief material.'' Santana worked in another leather-goods factory from February to July of 1968, quitting because of ''an injury to my arm.'' Mrs. Santana says that Santana quit or was fired from all three of his factory jobs because of his drinking. Santana didn't work regularly thereafter, alternately claiming ill health or inability to find a job, and the Santanas' home life deteriorated rapidly. In 1969, Santana began to desert his family for several months at a time, returning for a few truculent weeks only to leave again. Mrs. Santana says — Santana remains uncommunicative — that in 1967 or 1968 Santana borrowed some money from a loan shark, and that from then on whatever money he got that he didn't spend on beer was turned over to the loan shark. She saw almost nothing of his Home Relief check, and he often pawned the two-party rent check, so she had to provide for the family out of her Aid to Dependent Children check and her numbers earnings — on the occasions when Santana hadn't made off with those, too. Santana, she says, had always had a terrible temper, but his disposition took a turn for the worse after he fell into debt. The case record tends to confirm this. "Mrs. Santana was in the hospital undergoing a tonsillectomy," a caseworker wrote on June 26, 1969. "During the worker's visit the estranged husband of client was looking after the needs of the household. He was extremely brutal and almost violent with the children. He should never be permitted or allowed to have the children trusted with him." For a long time, Mrs. Santana kept the fact that she often had to borrow food to feed the children — "some rice from one relative, some lard from another" — from the Department of Social Services (as the Department of Welfare was renamed in 1967). Finally, she confronted Santana in the presence of a caseworker, whose account of a September 17, 1969, visit reads:

Mrs. Santana declares that she wants to find another apartment and she is trying to get another one and she is not going to stay with Mr. Vicente Santana . . . because Mr. Santana gives her too much trouble and too many problems staying out all night drinking . . . The problem is that Mrs. Santana declares that Mr. Santana refuses to give her the biggest part of the check for the family. He spends most of the money and he leaves not much for her to take care of the house. The food is never enough and she has trouble getting the money from him in order to pay a Con Edison bill. The problem of the relationship concerns the management of the money, and Mrs. Santana asked the Worker in front of Mr. Santana to have the Department send the biggest part of the money to her so he wouldn't spend too much money. At this Mr. Santana started an argument, and the Worker asked him not to talk because it would degenerate into a bigger argument . . . Clients have no resources whatsoever except the welfare check that they receive every 2 weeks. It is being recommended that Clients be kept on welfare rolls and it is recommended also that the biggest part of the check be sent out to Mrs. Santana because it is obvious that Mr. Santana spends all the money. If he were giving the money in a sufficient amount to his wife, this woman would not complain; therefore, Worker recommends that this part of the money be turned over to Mrs. Santana. At this time of the dictation Worker is informed that Mr. Vicente Santana has left for Puerto Rico from Kennedy Airport . . . Mrs. Santana has informed the Worker of this. Therefore, it is recommended that Mr. Santana, having left for Puerto Rico without informing the Worker, be removed from the welfare rolls.

Santana is scarcely mentioned in the case record after this, though Mrs. Santana's troubles with him were far from over. He remained in Puerto Rico only a few days, and he was furious to find upon his return that "his" check was now in Mrs. Santana's name, and quarreled with her about this. He came to the apartment a number of times, smashed up the furniture, scattered dirty clothes and garbage all over the living room, and then accused her of being a pig for living in such squalor. Earlier in the year, during one of Santana's prolonged absences from their apartment, Mrs. Santana had begun an affair with Francisco Delgado, a widower who had recently arrived in New York from Puerto Rico and was living nearby with a cousin. She had met Delgado while she was selling numbers on the streets of the lower East Side. Santana felt no compunction about his own comings and go-

ings, and made no attempts to conceal his infidelities —
Mrs. Santana once hit him with a pan after he stayed out all
night — but he was jealous of Mrs. Santana's relationship
with Delgado. He told a neighbor to "take my wife and do
whatever you want with her — she's a whore who will sell
her favors for a box of Chiclets." On one occasion, Santana
saw Delgado patting Mrs. Santana's arm on the street and
told him to get his hands off his wife, and then started a fist
fight; Delgado trounced him. On another occasion —
Mother's Day of 1970 — Mrs. Santana's two eldest sons,
Rafael and Felipe Rodríguez, gave Santana two black eyes
for making their mother's life so miserable in general and for
spoiling her Mother's Day in particular. In the summer of
1971, Mrs. Santana and her children quietly left their apartment and moved a few blocks away, to the apartment of
Rafael's wife. A few blocks is a long distance on the lower
East Side, but Santana eventually traced Mrs. Santana and
continued to pester her. In September of 1971, Mrs. Santana
decided it would be best to put a substantial barrier of space
between herself and Santana; although she preferred living on
the lower East Side near her older children, she moved with
Delgado and the four younger children to Brooklyn. Santana
didn't pursue her.

One of the two main problems in the Santana household
has always been money. The other was Santana's treatment
of Mrs. Santana's children by her first two husbands. From
the time Inocencia Castillo was eleven, Santana made sexual
advances to her. He expressed his resentment of Felipe Rodríguez, who always took his mother's side during quarrels,
by beating him and by denying him food. When Casilda and
Rafael Rodríguez came to New York in the mid-sixties (until
then they had lived elsewhere with their father and their step-

mother), he begrudged them food and made them unwelcome in the Santana apartment. Santana often cooked a meal, ate what he wanted, and spit or urinated in any food that was left over. He sometimes threw the pots and pans he had used out the window, leaving no cooking utensils for anyone else, and on several occasions he put a lock on the refrigerator. Not surprisingly, Mrs. Santana's children by Rafael Rodríguez and Angel Castillo always refer to Santana as "that bastard." Nor are the four Santana children very fond of their father. They sometimes go to see him on the lower East Side, where he now lives in disharmony with another woman and her children by other men, and succeed in cadging a dollar or two from him, but they seem to prefer Francisco Delgado. "Francisco buys us clothes and gives us good presents," Gabriel says. "My father was a pain in the neck. He gave us nothing but trouble."

The Department of Social Services has never attempted to get Santana, who works periodically, to contribute to the support of Vicente, Emilio, Gabriel, and María — maybe because it is understaffed, maybe because its searches for Puerto Rican ex-husbands (whose ex-wives are reluctant to borrow trouble by volunteering their addresses) are rarely fruitful. Mrs. Santana is not the sort of person to bear a grudge. Once Santana had found himself a new woman, he lost interest in harassing her; they nod to each other when they happen to meet on the street nowadays. Still, she acknowledges that he was by far the worst husband she has ever had. "I don't know why I put up with him all those years," she says. "He must have had me under a spell. I've been much better off since I moved to Brooklyn with Francisco."

O N the fifth and the twentieth of every month, Mrs. Santana receives a check from the Department of Social Services for two hundred ninety-four dollars. Of that sum, eighty-five dollars is for half of her rent (she pays a hundred seventy dollars a month for her four-room apartment), and the remaining two hundred nine dollars is the semimonthly grant given to a welfare family of seven people in New York City. Twice a month, Mrs. Santana is also sent the authorization to buy one hundred fifteen dollars' worth of food stamps. She is able to buy the stamps for seventy-six dollars. Mrs. Santana is cheating the Department of Social Services in two ways. She still receives support for her daughter Inocencia and Inocencia's first child, who was born in April of 1972, although they haven't lived with her since September of 1972. Instead of the grant for seven, Mrs. Santana should be getting only the New York City grant for a family of five, which is one hundred fifty-nine dollars every two weeks, plus authorization to buy food stamps. (Her food-stamp authorization would be for eighty-nine dollars; that amount of stamps would cost her fifty-seven dollars.) And she has not told the Department of Social Services that she is living with Francisco Delgado, who earns about a hundred fifty dollars a week working in a factory that makes automobile supplies. If the Department of Social Services were aware of Delgado's existence, it would not hold him responsible for supporting Mrs. Santana (because he isn't legally married to her) or her children (because he isn't their natural father), but it would attempt to make him liable for his share —

a sixth — of the rent. Mrs. Santana would also be asked to declare whatever money he gave her as income, and that sum would be deducted from her welfare check. Mrs. Santana has no qualms about "cheating on the welfare." Almost everyone she knows cheats on the welfare. Most of her friends are cheating by continuing to live with men — who in most cases hold jobs and have fathered some of their children — after claiming that the men have deserted them. Other friends have undeclared incomes of their own: some have regular factory jobs, some sell cosmetics from door to door. A while back, one of Mrs. Santana's former caseworkers asked eighteen welfare mothers whether they were cheating on the welfare. All eighteen trusted him sufficiently to tell the truth. Twelve of the eighteen admitted that they had unreported incomes. Although the caseworker knows that welfare-cheating enrages middle-class workers and threatens to destroy the entire welfare system, he is not inclined to turn anyone in for cheating. "You can't stop the cheating until you give people decent grants," he says. "Welfare grants haven't kept up with inflation in recent years, so a lot of the cheating today is justified. For instance, between September of nineteen seventy and December of nineteen seventy-three, while food prices increased thirty-three and a half percent here, welfare grants decreased ten percent." Mrs. Santana considers the welfare grants inadequate. "Welfare gives you only enough money for food and rent," she says. "It's not enough to live on." Mrs. Santana knows of a few women who struggle to get by on just their welfare grants. She doesn't regard their honesty and thrift as virtues, because "they have to do without so much."

Despite the fact that Delgado buys his breakfast and lunch

at work, and despite the fact that the four Santana children are entitled to free breakfasts and lunches at school, Mrs. Santana spends almost as much on food and household supplies as her entire legal grant for a family of five would be. Her semimonthly bill is never less than a hundred thirty dollars and sometimes runs as high as a hundred ninety dollars because her grown children and grandchildren eat at her apartment often. If Mrs. Santana knew as much about home economics as the people who draw up welfare budgets, and if she shopped judiciously once a week at the supermarket across the street from her apartment building, she could spend far less. Instead, she frequents a bodega a few doors away from the supermarket, and with good reason: when she runs out of money between welfare checks, as she inevitably does, the bodega will give her credit and the supermarket won't. There are no giant economy sizes, no specials, no money-saving house brands at the bodega, where prices of most items are about twenty percent higher than at the supermarket, but it has not been Mrs. Santana's experience that saving a few dollars on groceries has appreciably affected her situation.

Mrs. Santana shops the way Puerto Ricans have for generations — meal by meal and sometimes item by item. Early in the morning, she sends one of the children over to the bodega (after María's birth, Mrs. Santana began to suffer from chronic bronchitis, and she doesn't like to go up and down stairs any more than necessary) to buy whatever she thinks she will need for breakfast and lunch: half a pound of Bustelo coffee, a quart of milk, a loaf of Italian bread, a quarter of a pound of sliced ham, a quarter of a pound of sliced cheese, some margarine or mayonnaise, a bottle of

Pepsi-Cola. If her children come home for lunch because they don't like the free meal the school is serving and she runs out of something, she sends them across the street to charge another loaf of bread, another quart of milk. After lunch, she buys whatever she thinks she will need for dinner. The children are constantly in and out of the bodega during the afternoon and evening — it is one of their main activities — charging snacks (potato chips, cupcakes, soda, ice cream) or replacements for whatever the household has just run out of: two rolls of toilet paper, a small bottle of cooking oil, a box of soap powder.

On the mornings of the fifth and the twentieth of the month, Mrs. Santana waits at her mailbox in the hall for the mailman to bring her welfare check. On a recent twentieth of the month, the mailman appeared at ten with two pieces of mail for Mrs. Santana. One was her welfare check, the other a letter from the public school attended by Vicente and Emilio saying that they were to be suspended the following week for "dangerous behavior." The letter asked her to come in at the end of the week, with the boys, to "discuss ways to improve their behavior so that they may be returned to school." Mrs. Santana put the two envelopes in her pocketbook and set off immediately for a check-cashing place several blocks from her house, where she waited in line for fifteen minutes. Since the Department of Social Services has stopped sending out all welfare checks on the first and the sixteenth of the month and started staggering the checks, in an attempt to cut down on check-stealing, the line was much shorter than it used to be. Mrs. Santana paid a dollar and fifty-seven cents to have her check cashed. At the same time, she bought two fifty-cent New York State Lottery tickets. There is a bank in her neighborhood that would cash her check free of charge, but it is a few blocks farther away. As soon as she had the money in hand, she put eighty-five dollars for the rent in a separate compartment of her pocket-book. Her landlord's representative has made it his business to master the new welfare-check schedule, and he never fails to appear on the mornings of the sixth and the twenty-first of the month to collect the rent. Since her move to Brooklyn, Mrs. Santana has always paid her rent on time, except when something in the apartment is broken and she withholds the rent money as a means of persuading the landlord to repair it. Mrs. Santana also put aside twenty-four dollars to reimburse three acquaintances — her numbers man, her superintendent, a neighbor — from whom she had borrowed five dollars, fourteen dollars, and five dollars to get through the previous week. She walked from the check-cashing place to the bo-dega. There the proprietor greeted her cordially, turned to the pages of his account book listing all the items the family had charged in the past fifteen days, and told her that her bill came to one hundred sixty dollars and fifty cents. Mrs. San-tana sighed, because it was more than she had expected, and scanned the charges. One item — "Seven dollars cash" — displeased her. A few days earlier, she had dispatched Ga-briel to the bodega to borrow five dollars; he had obviously asked for seven dollars, given her five dollars, and kept two dollars for himself. She shook her head and told the propri-etor she would deal with Gabriel when he came home from school. She gave the proprietor her food stamps, and he deducted one hundred fifteen dollars from her account, leav-ing her with a new balance of forty-five dollars and fifty cents. Mrs. Santana never entirely wipes out her old balance

on check days, but this was a higher balance than she wanted
to have. Mrs. Santana's numbers man hangs out at the bodega. On her way out of the store, she gave him the five
dollars she owed him and three dollars to play on three different numbers. Mrs. Santana likes to play the numbers.
She plays them every day that she is solvent and some days
that she isn't. She has never kept track of how much she
spends playing the numbers in the course of a year, and so
cannot compare that figure with her annual winnings, but she
is happy each time she wins a small amount, and can cite
every number on which she has won big — three hundred
dollars or five hundred dollars — during the past three years.
She also remembers the dreams she has had that prompted
her to consult a dream book for proper numerical interpreta-
tions. Mrs. Santana has never saved a penny of her three-
hundred-dollar and five-hundred-dollar winnings, but the
windfalls have always been pleasant while they lasted. She
has used the money for new linoleum, clothes for herself and
the children, jewelry, beer and liquor for parties, trips to
Puerto Rico, and deposits on new furniture.

From the bodega Mrs. Santana slowly walked four blocks
(her bronchitis was bothering her, and she put the inhaler
she always keeps in her pocketbook to her mouth) to a large
furniture store. In June of 1974, she had dreamed about
eggs, had learned from the dream book that 465 was the
appropriate number to play when one had egg dreams, and
had won five hundred dollars on 465. She had made a
down payment of one hundred twenty-three dollars and
ninety-five cents of her winnings on a washing machine, a
coffee table, a lamp, a sofa, two easy chairs, and three plastic covers. The furniture cost a total of eight hundred sev-

enty-three dollars and ninety-five cents, leaving a balance, including interest, of seven hundred fifty dollars, which she had been instructed to pay off at the rate of forty dollars a month. One payday in October of 1974, Delgado made a down payment of forty-two dollars and forty-five cents on a bed, a dresser, and a wardrobe costing a total of two hundred ninety-two dollars and forty-five cents, the balance of which was to be paid off at the rate of twenty dollars a month. Social reformers decry the exorbitant rates of interest charged in New York City's slums by furniture stores that sell on credit to poor blacks and Puerto Ricans, but Mrs. Santana doesn't even know how much of the two large purchase prices represent interest charges. The figures aren't broken down in her furniture-payment books, and she knows only the total purchase prices and the balances owed. Nor does Mrs. Santana resent having to make payments on furniture that is already worn out; she blames her children and grand-children for the furniture's poor condition, rather than its shoddy construction. All her friends and relatives have the same sort of living room sets she has, protected by the same sort of plastic covers. Mrs. Santana likes furniture. As soon as she can afford the down payment on a new set, she looks forward to replacing her green and gold sofa and her aqua and gold and green and gold chairs with three almost iden-tical orange and gold and red and gold pieces. It has never occurred to Mrs. Santana to save, go to a department store, pay cash, and obtain better value for her money; large depart-ment stores confuse her, and, besides, she has never suc-ceeded in saving money for anything. The clerk to whom Mrs. Santana handed thirty dollars and her two furniture books recorded the payments in the books noncommittally.

When Mrs. Santana recently skipped two payments in a row, no one at the store expressed concern over the missed payments or threatened to repossess the furniture — no doubt because it wasn't worth repossessing. Mrs. Santana has never worried when she has been short of cash and couldn't meet a payment. When she has had the money, she has paid; otherwise, not.

By the time Mrs. Santana left the furniture store, she had seventy-three dollars and forty-three cents in her pocketbook to cover the next fifteen days. Cash would be needed for food and other household supplies that the bodega didn't stock; for playing the numbers; for spending money for the children, who are always clamoring for a peseta (quarter) here, a peso (dollar) there; for transportation, most of her trips being either to her welfare center (where she has frequent business to attend to) or to the lower East Side (to visit friends and relatives); for emergency loans to friends and relatives (one has to be prepared to lend money to friends and relatives whenever one can, so that one can borrow money from them whenever one has to); and for a visit to the beauty parlor. Mrs. Santana dislikes her frizzy hair, and has it straightened and set as often as possible. Whenever she calls a person ''handsome,'' like her second husband, Angel Castillo, the person's characteristics invariably include ''good'' hair — that is, hair that is straight.

Mrs. Santana's remaining cash wouldn't be sufficient to cover those expenses, much less the expenses Delgado usually took care of. Delgado's paychecks average a hundred and fifty dollars a week. He sends thirty dollars a week to his four children, who live back home in Yauco with his late wife's mother, and keeps a certain amount of money for his personal expenses — carfare, meals at work, clothes, cigarettes, beer, marijuana. He pays the gas-and-electricity bill and the phone bill. (The basic monthly charge for the phone is only seven dollars, but Mrs. Santana's older children often travel and call her long distance collect, so the phone bill sometimes runs as high as sixty dollars a month.) Each payday, he usually gives Mrs. Santana fifty dollars for the coming week for clothes for herself and the children, and for miscellaneous items. On a recent Friday evening, he gave her twenty dollars instead of the customary fifty. She didn't know why and didn't ask any questions.

From the furniture store, Mrs. Santana headed home along Havemeyer Street, one of Williamsburg's main shopping thoroughfares. It is a street lined with small Jewish, Puerto Rican, and Italian shops, which sell clothes, candy, pizza, cheese, fish, liquor, hardware, furniture, fruit and vegetables, and religious statues and other crockery bric-a-brac. In the streets of Mrs. Santana's neighborhood, in the late morning, children who should have been in school amused themselves by jumping on discarded mattresses; young men who could have been working souped up the motors of their Chevrolets or ogled the young women who sauntered along in three-somes and foursomes, inviting their attention; mothers wea-rily pushed their infants' strollers and held on to their tod-dlers' hands; scruffy mongrels foraged in the ubiquitous mounds of garbage, and stray cats suddenly ran out from under parked cars and from behind abandoned appliances; drug addicts shot up in vacant lots; heroin pushers went in and out of a local candy store, undisturbed by the cops on the beat, who were presumably being paid off not to disturb them; old men sipped from bottles wrapped in brown bags, or slept off last night's drunk on the sidewalk. Whenever Mrs. Santana spotted an acquaintance in the crowded street, she told her about her bodega bill, successfully soliciting her sympathy over the high cost of feeding a family. As she walked home, she looked longingly at the brightly-colored pants suits and see-through nightgowns in the windows of the clothing stores. Mrs. Santana has never subscribed to a magazine, owned a car, a rug, or an air conditioner, or bought insurance, but she and her children love clothes and spend about two thousand five hundred dollars a year to dress themselves in the latest styles. Mrs. Santana doesn't spend much on any single item for herself — her dresses cost about twelve dollars apiece — but the pegs in her bedroom hold an extensive collection of slacks, blouses, Bermuda shorts, sweaters, dresses, and satin undergarments. Mrs. Santana has been invited to attend the christening of Delgado's sister's baby. She doesn't look forward to going, because she may not have the money for a new long dress, and the other people who can be expected to attend have already seen all her other long dresses. Just as a light rain began to fall, Mrs. Santana stopped in at a small furniture store a block away from her apartment to look at a forty-dollar wardrobe she had priced many weeks earlier. She has never lived in a place that had closets, and her children had wrecked the last wardrobe she bought — the one on which she is still making payments — months ago. She hoped to have a spare forty dollars to replace the wardrobe before long, but she didn't have it then; perhaps she would hit a good number soon. Her last stop of the morning was at the bodega, where she charged a large white votive candle to her account.

As soon as Mrs. Santana was back inside her apartment, she consulted the fourteen-carat-gold Bulova watch Delgado had given her the previous Mother's Day. She seemed relieved that she had returned home in time to watch her favorite Spanish-language TV *novela,* which began at noon. She swallowed some cough medicine, turned on the living room television set Delgado had bought some months before from a man on the street for fifty dollars, without inquiring into its provenance, and settled into one of her frayed armchairs. She watched the latest episode of the *novela* with her customary enthusiasm.

The *novela* installment was followed by a news program. Mrs. Santana turned off the TV, turned on the phonograph to its top volume, and went into the kitchen. At the dinette table, she brushed away a cluster of cockroaches that sat boldly on half a loaf of Italian bread and two small packages of cheese and ham remaining from breakfast, fixed herself a hero sandwich, poured a glass of Pepsi-Cola, and sang along with the popular Spanish crooner whose latest record she was playing. Local human-interest stories — a subway crime, a rape, a sex murder — sometimes caught Mrs. Santana's fancy; most national and international news stories did not. Mrs. Santana rarely watches the news on television or buys a newspaper. She didn't vote for Nixon or ''the other one'' in the last presidential election, didn't favor either side in the Arab-Israeli Yom Kippur War, and didn't watch the Watergate hearings. ''The Watergate? I don't know what happened over there,'' she says. She was opposed to the Viet-

nam War — although she says she doesn't know what
happened over there, either — because she had heard that
many Puerto Rican soldiers were killed in the fighting. Five
years ago, she had worried that her son Rafael, who spent a
few months in the Army before going AWOL, would be sent
to Vietnam.

At one, Mrs. Santana's oldest daughter, Casilda, phoned
from the lower East Side to discuss the noon *novela* episode
and to bring her mother up to date on her own life, which of
late had contained enough dramatic incidents for several *novela* installments. At twenty-seven, Casilda looks and acts
very much her mother's daughter. She is gravely overweight
(she stands five-five and weighs two hundred and fourteen
pounds) but very attractive. She, too, married young in
order to escape from an unhappy home. In 1953, when
Casilda was five, she had flown with her brother Rafael from
Puerto Rico to Detroit to live with their father, Rafael Rodríguez; his second wife, Fulgencia; and two children that
Fulgencia Rodríguez had had by two different men between
the time she went out with Rafael Rodríguez in Cayey in
1946 and the time she met up with him in New York seven
years later. Fulgencia Rodríguez lavished clothes, toys, and
affection upon her own two children. She bought Casilda
and Rafael only the necessities and disciplined them harshly.
Casilda was made to help with the cooking, the cleaning, and
the laundry. Her stepsister was not required to help with the
household chores. Rafael Rodríguez earned a good living as
a mechanic in Detroit, but one day in 1963 he decided to
move back to Cayey; he reached this decision as abruptly as
he had reached the decision to leave Cayey for New York.
When Casilda started the tenth grade in Cayey, in September

of 1965, she was planning to finish high school and become a beautician. A month later, she met Roberto Figueroa, a trim, eighteen-year-old, seventh-grade dropout, who worked in his parents' small meat business. Fulgencia Rodríguez disapproved of Casilda's going out with young men. She didn't permit Roberto Figueroa, who had the reputation of being a playboy, to come to the house. In mid-December, the seventeen-year-old Casilda eloped with Roberto Figueroa. They spent a week at his parents' house in Cayey. At the end of the week, Rafael Rodríguez forced the young couple to marry. Casilda Rodríguez and Roberto Figueroa were married on November 25, 1965, in a Catholic church, in a double ceremony with Roberto's older brother, Reynaldo Figueroa, who was to get Casilda's then seven-year-old sister Inocencia Castillo pregnant six years later.

"We were married and lived unhappily ever after," says Casilda, who is given to exaggeration and to borrowing the language of true-confessions magazines, which she likes to read. "Ever after" was two and a half years. Casilda and Roberto Figueroa lived unhappily in Cayey, in Dover, New Jersey, and in New York, where Casilda was reunited with her mother after a ten-year separation, and where the Figueroas' daughter, Helen, was born on August 22, 1966, almost exactly nine months after the elopement. Roberto Figueroa had trouble keeping a job in New York, because he knew almost no English, so the Figueroas applied for welfare and received checks to supplement his meager and erratic wages. Wherever they lived, Roberto was unfaithful to Casilda and beat her when she complained about his philandering. In the fall of 1968, the Figueroas separated. Casilda kept Helen and applied for welfare on her own. She has been on welfare ever since. Among the financial resources Casilda has successfully concealed from the Department of Social Services are occasional earnings from selling numbers and holding jobs (packer in a shirt factory, clerk in a discount store) and income provided by Jesús Manrique, a handsome man of thirty-two, with whom she had been living since 1969. Shortly after Jesús Manrique, Jr., was born, in 1972, Casilda decided to report the birth of her baby and the fact that she was living with the baby's father to the Department of Social Services. She told an employee at her local welfare center that Jesús Manrique was earning ninety dollars a week at an electrical-appliance factory and was giving her about sixty dollars a week toward the household expenses. Casilda figured that if the welfare paid their rent, one hundred eight dollars a month, she and Jesús could get by without her welfare check. The worker calculated that Casilda and Jesús had a budget deficit of only eighty-four dollars a month, and informed Casilda that she would be receiving thirty-nine dollars every two weeks toward the rent. For two months, the thirty-nine dollar semimonthly checks failed to arrive. Casilda had to spend two days out of every fifteen at the local welfare center tracking them down. After two months of having to go to the welfare center and of being unable to make ends meet, Casilda came to the conclusion that honesty didn't pay, and reported that Jesús had deserted her. Since then, she has been receiving the grant for a family of three and her entire rent.

For six years, Casilda had been content with her life with Jesús. Although he suffered from an ulcer and she found him an inadequate lover, he was quiet, neat, and handy around the house. He didn't beat her, and he treated Helen kindly. Casilda's contentment had ended a couple of months earlier, when she discovered that Jesús was having an affair. For a while, Casilda tried to pretend that the affair was not taking place. Though Jesús gave her less money on payday than had been his custom, she didn't protest. One of her friends, whose husband worked with Jesús, asked her why she phoned Jesús so often at the factory; she didn't reply that she hadn't been calling him at all, nor did she ask Jesús about the calls. When Jesús started coming home late at night, she didn't challenge his unconvincing alibis. But when an expensive-looking bottle of men's cologne appeared on Jesús's dresser, Casilda couldn't refrain from asking him where he had got it. He said he had bought it at the drugstore for four dollars. The next morning, she priced the cologne at the drugstore; it cost twelve dollars. That afternoon, before she could confront Jesús with the discrepancy, Casilda discovered a pile of love letters under the bedroom linoleum, where Jesús had hidden them. What particularly hurt her feelings, she told her mother, was that the author of the letters was Aida González, her next-door neighbor and supposedly a good friend. Aida visited Casilda practically every day while Jesús was at work, and often came by in the evening to see them both. The letters made it clear that Aida and Jesús had gone to elaborate lengths to keep the affair from Aida's husband. In one letter, Aida instructed Jesús to give a thirty-five-dollar ring he had bought for her to one of her trusted girl friends, who could then offer to sell it to Aida's husband at a low price; her husband would be sure to buy it for her, and she would thus be able to wear it without arousing his suspicions.

That evening when Jesús came home from work, Casilda

threw the letters at him and told him to leave. Later, when
Aida came to visit them, Casilda started to beat her up.
Jesús stopped her. He was unable to stop her from calling
Aida's husband to apprise him of the affair. Jesús tearfully
begged Casilda's forgiveness and sought to justify his conduct: Aida had flirted with him, and he had had to prove his
manhood by going to bed with her. He had bought her the
ring only because she had bought him the cologne. Casilda
accepted the rationale. "When a woman bothers a man, he
has no alternative but to act like a man," she says. Even her
mother considered her partly to blame for the affair: Casilda
had seen Aida making eyes at Jesús and hadn't taken action
immediately. Jesús agreed to stop seeing Aida and to move
with Casilda to another apartment, on East Sixth Street, six
blocks away from temptation. Partly at her mother's urging,
Casilda agreed to give Jesús a second chance. For two
months, Jesús was a model husband. He brightened up the
crumbling walls of their fifth-floor walkup with gold and
green–flocked Con-Tact paper, and he was properly jealous
when Casilda stayed out until four in the morning, playing
bingo at a friend's house. Jesús hadn't made love to her in
several weeks, and when Casilda finally persuaded him to do
so, she discovered that the affair had begun again. Jesús
didn't want to take off his T-shirt. Casilda took it off for
him. She immediately noticed a love bite on his chest.
When she tried to put a similar mark of affection on his neck,
he wouldn't let her. "Either I do what I want with you, like
Aida, or you can go!" Casilda had screamed. Jesús had ignored the ultimatum. For ten days, they had scarcely spo-
ken.

Now, Casilda said, her voice trembling, the climactic moment had arrived. For last night Jesús hadn't come home. Casilda had phoned him that morning at the factory and had been told that he hadn't shown up for work. She was calling to ask what her mother thought she ought to do. "Get drunk," Mrs. Santana said. In the days since the quarrel over the love bite, Casilda had picked out a prospective new husband, one Alfonso Ortiz. Mrs. Santana hadn't yet met Alfonso, but she didn't like anything Casilda had told her about him: he was three years younger than Casilda, he was unemployed, and his last wife had just thrown him out of the house. Mrs. Santana believed that Casilda would be better off staying with Jesús. Casilda didn't care for her mother's advice. "The trouble with you, *Mami,* is that you don't take life seriously," Casilda said. "Getting drunk won't help. I feel so low I could sink in a glass of water."

Mrs. Santana, on whom Casilda's histrionics were wasted, replied, "Casilda, the trouble with you is that you're just like me. You don't have good luck with men. Rafael Rodríguez left me with three children. He's stuck with his second wife for over twenty years. Angel Castillo had no money for me — he was just a field worker when I was with him. Now he's high up in the numbers business in Cayey and lives with his third wife in a fancy house."

This time, Casilda regretfully concurred with her mother. "When I was with Roberto Figueroa, we traveled around like gypsies and we had nothing," she said. "Now Roberto is selling heroin and he's already made twenty thousand dollars. I'm glad I never got around to divorcing him. If something happens to him, I'll be his legal widow."

Mother and daughter turned from Casilda's troubles to family gossip. Casilda had heard that Inés Pérez, Roberto

Figueroa's latest wife, was pregnant; Inés claimed that the baby was Roberto's, but Roberto was going around denying it. Casilda had also learned that Fulgencia Rodríguez's son, Martín, a Navy officer, had recently been transferred to Japan, where his wife had "a genuine maid." Mrs. Santana told Casilda that Vicente Santana had given his wife a severe beating; she had been seen on the street with numerous bruises. The latest news about other members of the large Rodríguez, Castillo, Santana, Delgado, Figueroa, and Manrique families kept Casilda and her mother on the phone for fifteen minutes longer.

RESTED from her conversation with Casilda — she had lain down on her bed while they talked — Mrs. Santana got up, put a large pot of beans on the stove to simmer, and mopped the floors. Her bed is always unmade and she never dusts, but she mops the apartment several times a day. She took a load of clean sheets, towels, and clothes out of the washing machine and hung them up to dry on lines that cobwebbed the living room and the narrow front hall. If it hadn't been raining, she would have used outside lines that link her windows to the fire escape of the burned-out building across the courtyard. She set the new white candle on a saucer, lighted the candle, and put saucer and candle on the bedroom floor in front of a small table covered with china figures that Delgado and the children had given her over the years. On the table were two plump Buddhas, the head of an American Indian (Mrs. Santana believes that Buddhas and Indians bring good luck), and statues of Christ, St. Barbara, and St. Martín de Porres, a seventeenth-century half-caste, who is her favorite saint. Her son Rafael was supposed to drive from Dover, New Jersey, to New York that day. The last time he had made the trip, it had rained and he had wrecked his car. Mrs. Santana feared for his safety. The candle was her appeal to St. Clara, the patroness of good weather, childbirth, and television, to stop the rain. Rafael had spent the past year shuttling between two wives. One wife — Diana López, eighteen, a niece of Casilda's ex-husband, Roberto Figueroa, and of Inocencia Castillo's husband, Reynaldo Figueroa — was currently living in Dover. The other — Rosa Cruz, a sixteen-year-old former classmate of Inocencia Castillo's — lived in Brooklyn. Rafael had recently been taken into the heroin business by Roberto Figueroa. With part of his earnings, he had rented and furnished apartments for both his wives.

Shortly after two, Gabriel Santana bounded into the apartment. He had been released from school an hour early to attend a catechism class. He finds religious-instruction classes dull and usually cuts them. His mother doesn't care. She lights an occasional votive candle, and on welfare and hospital forms that ask for her religion she states that she is a Catholic, but she attends Mass only at Christmas and Easter, and doesn't hold the clergy in high esteem. "Once the priests started marrying, we saw that they were just as bad as the rest of us," she says. Mrs. Santana could just as accurately have put on the forms that she is a spiritualist, for she believes in the efficacy of curses and spells. It was a spell that had made her leave her favorite husband, Angel Castillo (she suspected his mother of having cast it), and a spell that had made her remain with Vicente Santana, her least-favorite husband, for ten years. Gabriel remembered that it was the twentieth of the month, and asked his mother for the money she had promised to give him on check day for a karate outfit. He had forgotten that check day would be his day of reckoning. He looked puzzled and then sheepish when his mother accused him, at the top of her voice, of misappropriating two dollars from the bodega. Gabriel made no excuses. He carefully put a row of Delgado's mod drip-dry shirts and flared slacks between him and his mother.

When Mrs. Santana is angry, she often swats her children; they have learned to keep their distance and remain silent until her anger subsides. Gabriel is considered by his mother the best-looking of the four Santana children. Emilio, Vicente, and María have inherited their parents' mulatto complexions, broad noses, puffy lips, and kinky hair. Gabriel bears a closer resemblance to Vicente Santana's white father and to Mrs. Santana's white grandfather. He has fine features, wavy black hair, and light skin. He is taller and slimmer than his older brothers. Gabriel is also the most highstrung and temperamental of the Santana children. When someone says something that offends him, he becomes enraged and throws the nearest available object at the offender. (He is still greatly admired within the family for having had the nerve to throw a can of corn at his father in 1969.) He boasts of his light skin, taunting other members of the family for looking like blacks. When Mrs. Santana was pregnant with Gabriel, two-year-old Vicente had toppled over a rickety hall railing and fallen two floors, breaking a leg and requiring eight stitches in his head. She attributes Gabriel's nervousness to the shock she suffered over Vicente's fall. Several years ago, Mrs. Santana had been persuaded to take Gabriel to a hospital for neurological tests. She went to the hospital with him twice, but it was a long, tiring journey from her apartment and she stopped going before his condition had been diagnosed.

At three, María Santana came home from school in the company of her friend Lillian Alvarez, who had been waiting patiently on the front stoop for her for hours. Lillian's mother, Margie Mendoza, an Italian woman whose husbands have included blacks and Puerto Ricans, didn't believe the public schools were good enough for her three comely daughters. She couldn't afford to send them to parochial schools, so she let them stay home. María, a slender, ten-year-old tomboy with a fetching smile, the vocabulary of a roustabout, a habit of sucking her thumb, and a precocious knowledge of the facts of life (at the age of seven she had startled one of her mother's caseworkers by asking him, "Will you make me a baby?"), handed her mother a note she had been given at school and her notebook. Mrs. Santana read the note. It requested her to take María to an ophthalmologist for an eye examination. She put the notebook down on the coffee table without opening it. The notebook was filled with sentences that seemed to have little relevance to Puerto Rican life in New York City's slums. Among them were the sentences "Father takes the short road home" and "Mother and Father laughed at Billy and Bobby," which María had been told to copy ten times. María enjoys copying, and she had done her work neatly, misspelling "road" and "laughed" ten times apiece. At the top of the page she had printed "María do good work. María right good." The four Santana children speak fluent, albeit slangy and ungrammatical, English with a Spanish inflection, but they all have difficulty reading and writing English. María, the only Santana child who has never been suspended from school, is in 5–4, an average fifth-grade class. (The best is 5–1; the worst is 5–9.) She attends school about four days a week, receives satisfactory marks, and reads on a first-grade level.

Having decided to serve pork chops for dinner with the beans that had been simmering and the rice that she would soon put on to boil, Mrs. Santana sent María to the bodega with instructions to charge some pork chops to her account. María and Lillian returned in five minutes with a bag of Fritos, which they shared with Mrs. Santana and Gabriel, and the news that the bodega was out of meat — a situation that would have meant a meatless dinner on a day when there was no cash in the house. Mrs. Santana took five dollars from her pocketbook and told María to buy a package of pork chops at the supermarket. The Santanas prefer Puerto Rican food to American food. Their evening meal usually consists of rice and beans with chicken, dried codfish, or some part of a pig (pork chops, pigs' feet, pigs' knuckles, pigs' ears, pork heart). Mrs. Santana sometimes cooks crab or octopus. She rarely serves beef. She and her family like *yautías* (a variety of tuber) and *plátanos* (green bananas); they view green vegetables with alarm.

As soon as thirteen-year-old Vicente Santana turned up, at three-thirty, Mrs. Santana yelled at him about the suspension notice. Vicente did not look contrite. A stocky boy with a husky voice, he finds school boring and often plays hooky without his mother's knowledge. He once spent a summer picking tomatoes and lima beans near Dover (where Roberto and Reynaldo Figueroa's parents had bought a house), and he prefers field work to schoolwork. He also prefers women to book learning. When Vicente was twelve, Mrs. Santana caught him in her bed with Lillian Alvarez's older sister Delfina. His latest girl friend is sixteen years old and uses drugs. Mrs. Santana doesn't worry about Vicente's getting the girl pregnant — that is the girl's mother's concern — but she fears that the girl may get Vicente started on drugs. Mrs. Santana attributes her son Felipe Rodríguez's heroin addiction to his wife, Georgina Herrera, who is five years older than he and who was using drugs when they started living together four years ago. Mrs. Santana's anger with Vicente quickly waned. She asked him where his brother Emilio was. Vicente said that Emilio had gone straight from school to the lower East Side to see some friends. Three of Vicente's buddies came to the apartment looking for him. One of them said he was hungry. Vicente fixed him a margarine and jelly sandwich. The rain had stopped, with or without St. Clara's intervention, and the four boys ran off to play ball.

Despite Williamsburg's high crime statistics, Mrs. Santana isn't afraid of robbers and rapists, and locks her door only when no one is at home. For the next hour, her front door opened and closed several dozen times as the Santana children and their friends entered and left. Gabriel went out with his shoeshine box, earned fifty cents, and returned with a package of assorted foreign stamps he had bought for his stamp collection. Margie Mendoza, who is one of Mrs. Santana's very few non–Puerto Rican friends, stopped by to use the phone. The building superintendent came to repair a leaking faucet in the bathtub and to gossip. María and Lillian brought in a friend's new talking doll to show Mrs. Santana, who laughed even harder than the two ten-year-olds when she pulled its cord and the doll said, in a tinny voice, "Can you wiggle your nose? I can." Emilio, a self-contained, self-confident twelve-year-old, came home from the lower East Side and was briefly castigated for the suspension notice. He reported that he had visited Casilda and had found her in her apartment dancing with Alfonso. One of the children had turned on the television set, and it stayed on all afternoon. Mrs. Santana gave half her attention to her children's comings and goings and half to a quiz show. She didn't understand the questions and answers, but she admired the female contestants' dresses and hairdos and exclaimed over the sets of matched luggage, the strands of cultured pearls, and the trips for two to Hawaii that they won or failed to win. The quiz show was followed by a cartoon program; Mrs. Santana is an ardent fan of "Bugs Bunny," "The Flintstones," and "Huckleberry Hound."

At five, when Emilio and Vicente said they were hungry, Mrs. Santana rinsed off two forks and two plastic plates, put a pork chop on each plate, and surrounded the chops with rice and beans. The boys helped themselves to bread and soda and watched TV as they ate at the dinette table. Mrs. Santana prepared two more plates of food for Gabriel and María, who ate on the living room sofa. Francisco Delgado usually returned from the automobile-supply factory around five. He had cut his arm on a sharp-edged machine the previous week and had a five o'clock doctor's appointment that day, so Mrs. Santana put a large pork chop and a generous helping of rice and beans on a plate and set it aside for him. Delgado walked in at six-fifteen. Instead of kissing Mrs. Santana on the mouth, his customary greeting, he took thirty-five dollars out of his pocket and handed her the money, wordlessly. Mrs. Santana looked at the bills and stuffed them into her bra. "Tell him thank you," said Gabriel. Instead, Mrs. Santana reacted as she had when Delgado gave her twenty dollars instead of fifty the previous week; she said nothing. She put Delgado's plate of food down on the table, rinsed off the plate and the fork Vicente had used (the household is chronically short of cutlery and plasticware), and helped herself to a modest portion of rice and beans and the smallest of the three pork chops left in the pot. She sent Emilio to the bodega for a quart of beer for Delgado and sat down to eat. For a few minutes, Mrs. Santana and Delgado ate in silence. Delgado never tells Mrs. Santana about his work (she has only a vague notion of what he does at the automobile-supply company), and Mrs. Santana doesn't inform Delgado of the children's misdeeds. When they first set up housekeeping in Brooklyn, Delgado had tried to discipline the children, but he had quickly learned that Mrs. Santana didn't like anyone but herself to hit them or correct them. Presently, Mrs. Santana told Delgado what numbers she had played that day (an hour later, the numbers man stopped by to inform her that she hadn't won), and passed along some of the gossip she had acquired from Casilda, Margie Mendoza, and the superintendent. Mrs. Santana and Delgado had just finished eating when her son Felipe Rodríguez walked in, accompanied by five scruffy, weary-looking children.

The four older children, ranging in age from four to eight, were Georgina Herrera's by two other men; the baby was Felipe and Georgina's year-old son, Felipe Rodríguez, Jr., called Junito. Felipe and Georgina had been evicted from their apartment in Williamsburg several days before for non-payment of rent. They had paid the rent, but their landlord hadn't cashed their check, because, as Georgina put it, he "had this fucking prejudice against drug addicts." They had found an apartment on the lower East Side and were living more or less on the streets until they could move in. Mrs. Santana saw the children staring at her empty plate and sent María to the bodega for a jar of baby food for Junito. She rinsed off four plates, divided up the two pork chops and the last of the rice and beans, and handed the plates to the four older children. She heated the jar of strained spaghetti María had fetched for Junito, took him on her lap, and fed him. Junito finished his meal quickly, which pleased Mrs. Santana; in her family a fat baby is much more highly regarded than a thin one. She sent María back to the bodega for a second jar of baby food and a box of Pampers. After Junito had bolted a jar of puréed macaroni, María changed his diaper. She and Lillian then took Georgina's four-year-old daughter, Dorothy, downstairs. They were proud of Dorothy's bilingual vocabulary of four-letter words and her ferocious knack for biting other children, and they wanted to show her off to their friends.

Felipe Rodríguez, a short, very slight man of twenty-two, with narrow eyes, a mustache, an Afro, and a dark complexion, had declined his mother's offer of food. For the past four years, he has shown little interest in eating, or in anything except drugs. In a voice that was slurred and barely audible, Felipe said he had come up to the apartment to take a bath, and shuffled to the bathroom like a sleepwalker. Mrs. Santana doesn't want her younger children to follow Felipe's example; she refuses to let him shoot up in their presence. In spite of the bad example he sets as an addict, she is always glad to see him and always speaks fondly of him. When he was seven, Felipe Rodríguez had flown from Puerto Rico to New York to join his mother and his new stepfather. Vicente Santana took an early dislike to Felipe for siding with his mother whenever they fought, and gave him frequent undeserved beatings. Santana often predicted that Felipe would drop out of school and become a drug addict — a prediction that Casilda believes was self-fulfilling. Felipe picked up English fairly easily after his arrival in New York, but he got off to a late start in school and never caught up. He was put in classes for slow learners and was kept back twice. In 1968, when he was repeating the seventh grade, he was told he would be kept back again. "Either promote me or I quit," he said. He was not promoted. He quit and got a job as a clerk in a bodega. Six months later, he was caught sniffing glue and was fired. In 1970, Mrs. Santana's caseworker prevailed upon Felipe to sign up for a Work Incentive Program administered by the New York State Department of Labor. His nine-to-five program consisted primarily of reading lessons. After a few months, Felipe was mistakenly dropped from the program — someone had got him mixed up with another Felipe Rodríguez — but by then Felipe had met Georgina and had had enough of the program anyway. "If I had to learn to read, why didn't they promote me and let me learn to read in ninth grade with my friends?" he says. "At least school let out at three. Reading until five! Man, that was one hell of a drag."

In 1971, Felipe moved in with Georgina Herrera, who was on welfare and on heroin. Before long, Felipe was snorting cocaine, then skinning heroin, then mainlining heroin. Georgina supports her habit — and Felipe's — by stealing and prostitution. Felipe remains at home and takes care of the children. Georgina is a versatile thief. She steals welfare checks from broken mailboxes and money from supermarket cash register drawers while the cashier's back is turned, but her specialty is shoplifting. When, as she says, she "needs" small items, she puts on a bulky coat with a special lining, enters a store, and comes out with a liningful of shoes, jewelry, or children's clothes. When she needs a large item, she goes to a store, picks up a sewing machine, a portable TV, or a coat, and boldly carries it out; so far, she has never been caught. Georgina has no more compunction about stealing from acquaintances than she has about stealing from strangers. Once, at a party at Casilda's house, she took another guest's welfare check from her purse; at a medical clinic she picked her doctor's pocket. Recently, Georgina stole a pair of María's earrings from Mrs. Santana's top bureau drawer. Mrs. Santana saw her superintendent's wife wearing some gold earrings and remarked that they looked exactly like the thirty-dollar earrings María's godmother had given her when she made her First Communion. The super's wife told Mrs. Santana that her husband had bought the earrings from Georgina for five dollars. Mrs. Santana bought them back, told Felipe what Georgina had done, and declared her apartment off limits to Georgina. The five dollars had helped buy a fix for Felipe, but Felipe would have lost face with his family if he had condoned a theft from his baby sister, so he gave Georgina a beating.

Georgina, who had been banned on a previous occasion for stealing one of Mrs. Santana's rings, took her obligatory beatings and banishments in stride. While her children ate dinner and her husband bathed, Georgina sat on the front stoop of the building and chain-smoked. There were dark circles under her hazel eyes, but she was alert and talkative with passersby. She had on a pair of rumpled blue jeans, a skimpy top that revealed the stretch marks on her stomach, and clunky shoes. She wore her dirty-blond hair in two bunches and looked younger than her twenty-seven years. Georgina and Felipe both speak openly about their drug addiction and about Georgina's stealing. Georgina is proud of her ability to march merchandise confidently past store guards; neither she nor Felipe feels that stealing is morally wrong. "In this world, you got to do everything — cheat, lie, whatever comes up — to live," Felipe says. His reasons for not wanting his children to steal are purely pragmatic: they might not be as good at it as their mother, and so might get caught. Georgina and Felipe are less forthright about Georgina's other sideline. Whenever Georgina stays out all night and returns with several hundred dollars, she tells Felipe that one of her stepfathers, a bail bondsman, gave her the money. Since Felipe chooses to accept the generous-stepfather lie, Mrs. Santana, who understands and respects the macho principle, is careful to look around the room and make sure that Felipe is not in it before she calls Georgina a whore. She and her older children have attempted to introduce Felipe to other women, in the hope that he will leave Georgina. They bad-mouth Georgina to their friends, and they insist to one another that they tolerate Georgina only because she is their well-loved Felipe's wife, but their attitude toward her shoplifting is ambivalent. Georgina recently stole a pair of sneakers that proved to be too small for Felipe. She offered them to Emilio. They fitted him perfectly, and he was happy to have them.

At 10:00 P.M., Felipe, Georgina, and the children de-
parted. Mrs. Santana told María, Gabriel, Emilio, and Vicente that it was time for bed. They continued going in and
out — to the bodega, to friends' apartments — as if they
hadn't heard her. An hour passed. Mrs. Santana raised her
voice and threatened them with a beating if they didn't go to
bed. The four children settled down in the living room,
where Delgado and Mrs. Santana were sitting on the sofa
drinking their third quart of beer and watching a nineteen-for-
ties movie. At one o'clock, Delgado got up, went into the
bedroom, and fell asleep on top of the unmade bed with his
clothes on. The apartment was still except for the melli-
fluous voice of Cary Grant, but that was often drowned out
by the crowing of roosters that were being raised for cock-
fights in cages on nearby fire escapes and by the smashing of
bottles thrown out of other people's windows. The children
climbed into their bunks at two-thirty. It was three o'clock
in the morning when Mrs. Santana changed into her
nightgown, in the dark, and lay down next to Delgado. She
immediately fell asleep.

D URING the week of Emilio's and Vicente's suspensions
from school, a neighborhood exhibitionist exposed himself to
Emilio and attempted to force him to commit fellatio, and a
local drug pusher gave Vicente a snort of cocaine. Mrs.
Santana is aware that the lower East Side is no more free of
sexual deviates and pushers than Williamsburg, but, having
made only a few friends in Brooklyn and having thought for
some time of moving back to the lower East Side to be closer

to the many friends and relatives she has there, she regarded
the boys' misadventures as an additional inducement.   When
Casilda mentioned to her on the phone one afternoon that
there was a five-room apartment in her building for rent at
one hundred ninety-five dollars a month, Mrs. Santana called
Casilda's landlord and told him she wanted the apartment.
Throughout the nineteen sixties, welfare clients like Mrs.
Santana had been permitted to move almost as often as they
pleased.   It had pleased many of them to move from one
tenement to another very often indeed; in 1968 Mrs. Santana
had moved four times.   When a welfare client moved, the
Department of Social Services usually paid for the moving
van and paid a one-month security deposit and a broker's fee.
To halt these frequent changes of residence at the taxpayers'
expense, the Department of Social Services had decreed in
1973 that unless a welfare client had an exceptional reason
for moving he or she would have to remain in a given apartment for a minimum of two years.   Mrs. Santana was well
aware of the two-year regulation; though she made no effort
to keep up with the news, she noted at once every change in
the welfare system.   Having been in her present apartment
for four years, she felt confident that she would be permitted
to move.

At nine o'clock one Thursday morning, Mrs. Santana set
off with Gabriel for her welfare office, in the Borough Hall
section of Brooklyn.   Whenever she had to go to a welfare
center, Gabriel stayed home from school to shepherd her up
and down the subway stairs and to keep her company.   At
the subway station a few blocks from her home, Mrs. Santana bought a token.   Until late 1968, welfare had provided
the money for travel to and from the center; then the travel
policy had been rescinded.   While no one was looking, Ga-

briel leaped over the turnstile; he and his brothers never pay
to ride the subway. At 9:45, after a three-subway-train journey, Mrs. Santana and Gabriel arrived at the welfare center.
They made their way to a large, crowded waiting room.
Mrs. Santana gave her name and case number to a recep-
tionist at the front desk. She and Gabriel found two empty
chairs in the back of the room and sat down. Most of the
hundred and fifty chairs in the room were occupied by young
and middle-aged black and Puerto Rican women and their
children. The babies slept, drank their bottles, and fussed.
The toddlers ran up and down the aisles sucking their paci-
fiers. Few of the women or the school-age children chatted,
and none of them read. They just sat, as Mrs. Santana and
Gabriel did, staring into space. At noon, Mrs. Santana gave
Gabriel some money to go out and buy himself a sandwich.
Mrs. Santana was low on funds, so she went without lunch.
At two, Mrs. Santana's name was called over a loudspeaker.
A stylishly dressed middle-aged woman led her to her desk,
told her to have a seat, and asked what had brought her in.
Mrs. Santana explained that she wanted to move from her
present four-room apartment in Brooklyn to a five-room
apartment on the lower East Side. The woman listened while
Mrs. Santana told her that her present rent was one hundred
seventy dollars a month, the new apartment would be one
hundred ninety-five dollars a month, the security deposit one
hundred ninety-five dollars, the broker's fee one hundred
ninety-five. After Mrs. Santana finished reciting these figures, the woman told her that no one had been able to find
her case record, that the rent sounded excessive to her, and
that she should return in a few days with some valid reason
for moving.

On the following Monday, Mrs. Santana and Gabriel returned to the welfare center. This time, after they had had another long wait, a male welfare worker escorted Mrs. Santana to his desk. He had her case record in hand, and he seemed more affable than the woman she had seen previously. When he asked her why she wanted to move, she said nothing about wanting to be nearer her friends and relatives. She just said that there were bad people in her building trying to foist drugs on her children. Years of dealing with the welfare had taught her what the welfare wanted to hear. The man nodded sympathetically. He didn't say that the rent was excessive — one hundred ninety-five dollars was below the maximum allowed for a family of seven, which was what the Santana family claimed to be. The welfare worker said that before he could approve the move Mrs. Santana would have to produce a two-year lease for the new apartment from the broker. On Tuesday morning, Mrs. Santana went to the broker's office on the lower East Side and obtained a two-year lease. She took it to the welfare center in the afternoon. Another worker — the third in a row that Mrs. Santana had never seen before — told her that, although the lease looked all right, she would have to bring in a copy of the broker's license before she could move. Mrs. Santana spent most of Wednesday obtaining a copy of the broker's license. She planned to return to the welfare center on Thursday, but she had bronchitis again and spent the day in bed. On Friday, it rained hard, so again she stayed home. A few days later, when she returned to the center, the man to whom she handed the copy of the broker's license reviewed the matter and informed her that she needed still another piece of paper: a declaration from the broker to the effect that there was no conflict of interest between him and the landlord — that he had no financial interest in the apartment building.

Mrs. Santana sighed and observed to the man that this was the fourth time she had come to the welfare center about the move. She wasn't complaining, she was just stating a fact. She had resigned herself to making yet another trip to the broker's office when the worker said to her, in a nasty tone, "I don't care if you have to come here fifteen times. It's not my problem. You people always think you can get something for nothing." Mrs. Santana is a cheerful, considerate, unmalicious woman. Most people with whom she comes in contact respond warmly to her good nature. She was unprepared for the man's harsh attitude, and was stunned by his harsh words. Impulsively, she tore up the broker's license, threw it into a nearby wastebasket, called the man the worst obscenities she could think of — in English, so he would be certain to understand them — and walked out of the center, thinking how much better the pre-1971 system of having a particular caseworker assigned to her had been than the present one of having to deal with a series of indifferent strangers. Mrs. Santana had not viewed the caseworkers' home visits as an invasion of her privacy. Unlike some of her friends on welfare, she had never been paid any postmidnight surprise visits by caseworkers checking up on her; on the contrary, her caseworkers had almost always dropped her letters to inform her in advance of their next visits, which always occurred between the hours of nine in the morning and five in the afternoon. She had had no trouble concealing from them whatever she wanted to conceal (her occasional factory jobs, her numbers activities and arrests), and she hadn't minded answering their personal questions; they were the only people who had ever asked her about herself. She hadn't minded listening to their advice, either, although she had rarely followed it. She had found the college-educated caseworkers far more responsive to her troubles than the high school-educated clerks she had had to go to the welfare center to see since 1971, when the caseworkers were transferred to other jobs.

When Casilda called her mother later in the day and learned that she was not going to move, she said she was sorry; actually, she was relieved. With Jesús absent (who knew for how long?), Casilda felt lonely. Thinking at first that it would be nice to have her mother nearby for company, she had told her about the apartment that had become available; then she had begun to fear that if her mother moved there and Jesús returned, her mother and her four undisciplined children, who would always be running in and out of Casilda's apartment and raiding her icebox, would get on Jesús's nerves and might drive him away permanently.

Mrs. Santana and Gabriel were back at the welfare center within twenty-four hours. In the process of trying to move, Mrs. Santana had received a letter that read:

> The employment section in your center is interested in helping you to find employment. An appointment has been arranged for you on . . . Please bring this letter, your NYSES registration book, and your Social Security card . . . You are expected to keep this appointment in compliance with the Social Services Law 131.4. If it is impossible for you to do so, please telephone me . . . Failure to do so or to communicate with this office may affect your continued receipt of public assistance.

The letter was signed by a man with the title of Employment Specialist, and the appointment was for 10:00 A.M. on the day following Mrs. Santana's unhappy confrontation with the welfare worker. Mrs. Santana wasn't troubled by the letter; she had received several similar letters in the course of the year. When she left the house, she took along a note that she had obtained some time earlier from a doctor she saw once or twice a week about her bronchitis.

There were no lines in the employment section, which was a floor below the main waiting room. A woman led Mrs. Santana in to see an employment specialist. Mrs. Santana handed him the letter she had received, her New York State Employment Service book, her Social Security card, and her doctor's note, which read, "Carmen Santana has severe bronchitis. She is not capable of doing hard physical work, nor can she work in a dusty environment." It took but a few seconds for the man to record the fact that Mrs. Santana had complied with Social Services Law 131.4 by keeping the appointment. He said, "Thank you very much for coming," and indicated that she was free to leave. Sometimes, when being on welfare seems more arduous than working, Mrs. Santana thinks about getting a job. The children are her main reason for not wanting to go back to work at present. She knows a number of women who have young children and who work. Their children run wild and get into far more serious trouble than Vicente, Emilio, Gabriel, and María do.

Mrs. Santana is unaware of the resentment felt by many taxpayers against people living on welfare. Her own attitude about being on welfare is clear. She doesn't feel embarrassed or degraded by it. For one thing, the majority of the people she knows are welfare recipients. For another, friends and relatives who have never been on welfare — her brother Jaime Ramírez, for instance — don't act as if they considered themselves superior to her because they have found jobs that enable them to support their families and she has not. Nor does she feel militantly pro-welfare; she has never joined a welfare-rights organization to demand increased benefits. She came to the United States in 1959 because salaries in New York were higher than salaries in Puerto Rico. She worked for two years and had no fault to find with her factory jobs. She learned about welfare only after she came to New York, and turned to it in 1961 only when she couldn't find a baby sitter she could afford on her salary and when her husband, Vicente Santana, was laid off. Mrs. Santana takes welfare as matter-of-factly as she takes everything else in her life. Although she has been the beneficiary of thousands of dollars of welfare for fourteen years, she doesn't consider welfare the only thing that stands between her and starvation. Because welfare exists, she avails herself of it. She believes that if there were no welfare she would find some means of surviving. Mrs. Santana thinks she will probably go back to work when María is grown. She has no idea what jobs there may be in New York City that will pay a living wage to a middle-aged Puerto Rican woman with an eighth-grade education who speaks so-so English, possesses no skills, and suffers from bronchitis. Other welfare mothers of her acquaintance regularly receive letters from employment specialists and don't have bronchitis, but they never receive job offers, so she suspects that jobs are scarce.

As a consequence of her many tiring trips to the local welfare center, Mrs. Santana didn't get around to having Emilio and Vicente reinstated in school at the end of their week's suspensions. Then, after the boys had enjoyed an extra ten days of liberty, Mrs. Santana set off with them for their school. The boys were uncharacteristically subdued during the five-block walk. "The teachers pick on us just because we're Puerto Rican," Vicente said, without much conviction, as they approached the school. A shrug of Mrs. Santana's shoulders served to indicate her skepticism. She knew — and she knew that Vicente knew — that ninety percent of the pupils in his school were Puerto Rican, and that some of them were A students and were never suspended.

At the school, Mrs. Santana gave her name to a secretary in the principal's anteroom. After ten minutes, she and the boys were ushered into the principal's office and invited to sit down at a long table with the principal, a benign-looking, bespectacled middle-aged man with an Italian surname. Also present was one of the school's guidance counselors, a pleasant-faced man of about thirty-five with a Jewish surname. The guidance counselor went right to the heart of the matter by reading the bill of complaints against Emilio that had resulted in his suspension: "Refused to sit down when teacher told the class to sit down, saying, 'Shit, I don't have to sit'; disruptive in class; deliberately whistled after told numerous times to be quiet. Threw milk on the floor of the lunchroom. Sent to detention class but no improvement in behavior there. No attempt to do any class assignments. Late to school twenty-three times without any explanation in last three months." With hardly a pause, the guidance counselor began to read the charges against Vicente, in a monotone, keeping his eyes on the piece of paper, so that they wouldn't meet Mrs. Santana's: "Sound asleep in class, snoring and drooling. Played with his hair, cracked his knuckles, molded clay into the shape of a penis. Laughed, yelled, moved the classroom furniture around. In detention class, showed pictures of a nude woman to other pupils, made the noise of a machine gun, sang, laughed out loud, seemingly without control.'' Vicente and Emilio betrayed no emotion as the charges were read. Mrs. Santana scowled and made a few grimaces of vexation.

The principal observed to Mrs. Santana that he had noticed that both of the boys yawned frequently and always looked exhausted. He asked her what their bedtime was. ''Well, I tell them to go to bed around nine o'clock, but they don't go,'' Mrs. Santana said. ''They stay up late — sometimes until midnight, sometimes one o'clock or two o'clock.'' The principal and the guidance counselor commented simultaneously that the boys ought to be in bed earlier. ''I tell them, sometimes I hit them,'' Mrs. Santana said. ''What else can I do?'' The guidance counselor turned to the problem of the boys' lateness for school. Mrs. Santana, who had had no idea until that morning that Emilio had been late twenty-three times in the last three months, told the counselor that Emilio left her house on time most mornings. She had assumed he went to school. At any rate, walking him to school would probably not have done much good. She had walked him to school one day the previous year when he said he hadn't felt like going, only to learn from Vicente that he had left school a few minutes later and had gone to Coney Island. The principal said that if Mrs. Santana found her children uncontrollable, she could take them to Family Court and have them declared PINS — Persons In Need of Supervision. He pointed out that this had the disadvantage of giving them a record with the court, and that the court could decide to remove them to a foster home. In some cases, he continued, sending problem boys away to a home had proved beneficial. Mrs. Santana shook her head. Occasionally, when Vicente and Emilio got her mad she threatened to send them away to a home, but it was an idle threat. She believed that sending children away only turned them against their mothers; besides, she would have missed them too much. Mrs. Santana attributed Georgina's stealing and whoring to the fact that she had spent her early years in foster homes, and that as a teen-ager she had been sent away to a school for wayward girls. The principal said that Vicente and Emilio might do better in a special day school for emotionally disturbed and socially maladjusted youngsters than in a neighborhood public school. Again Mrs. Santana shook her head. She said she had heard terrible things about special day schools. The principal's final suggestion was that something was physically wrong with the boys that accounted for their bad behavior. He asked Mrs. Santana if she would be willing to take them to a doctor to be examined, and told her that the doctor might prescribe tranquilizers for them, which might quiet them down. Mrs. Santana didn't believe there was anything physically wrong with her boys, but since she was as eager to end the session as the principal obviously was, she agreed to take the boys straight to the doctor. The principal asked her for the doctor's name and address, thanked Mrs. Santana for coming to see him, and dictated a note for the doctor to his secretary. While the secretary typed up the note, which requested the doctor to "give to both boys a complete physical examination and a possible referral for a psychiatric examination if necessary," Mrs. Santana noticed a woman sorting mail. As the women distributed letters to the teachers' mail slots, Mrs. Santana thought to herself that that was the sort of job she would like the employment specialist to find for her.

With the conference behind them, Vicente and Emilio became their rambunctious selves on the walk to the doctor, eight blocks away. They saw three teen-aged Chassidic Jewish boys across the street, ran over to them, tugged at their long side curls, and ran off, laughing. They went up to a big dog that was chained to a lamppost and teased it to make it bark and lunge at them. They saw a hot-dog vender and badgered their mother for hot dogs and sodas. (The previous week, on the lower East Side, Casilda had seen them steal money from a blind hot-dog vender.) They paused in front of a sporting-goods store and whiningly beseeched Mrs. Santana for combat boots, fatigue jackets, swimming trunks, a basketball, and a baseball. When she was in a good mood, she often said, "What the kids want I got to buy for them." Today, in answer to their pleading, she said sharply, "Money, money, money." Suddenly Emilio and Vicente told Mrs. Santana they had to go to the bathroom and couldn't wait. The look she gave them conveyed her disgust. As they started to relieve themselves at the curb, she walked on ahead, dissociating herself from them.

The doctor whom Mrs. Santana sees regularly about her bronchitis and the family's other health problems works in a clinic that occupies a modern one-story glass-and-brick building. About forty people — most of them welfare recipients with Medicaid cards that entitled them to free medical treatment — were seated on plastic chairs waiting to see the different doctors who worked at the clinic. The nurse-receptionists were all attractive young Puerto Rican women who greeted Mrs. Santana by name. After hearing about the school conference that had brought her in, one of them told her *she* didn't think that Vicente and Emilio were problem children, and another said, "Boys will be boys."

After waiting half an hour, Mrs. Santana was shown in to see her doctor, a young man who had chosen to spend a year in the clinic to acquire experience before moving to the suburbs and starting a private practice. The doctor, of whom Mrs. Santana is very fond and who seems very fond of her, asked her about her bronchitis. She told him she felt all right. She gave him the principal's note and told him that the principal wanted him to prescribe pills to quiet Vicente and Emilio down. The doctor frowned; the schools, he mumbled, half to himself, seemed to think they could drug away the effects that life in New York City's slums had on Puerto Rican children, instead of dealing with the conditions that caused their rowdy behavior. The doctor asked the boys to open their mouths and say "Ah." He examined their ears and eyes with an oto-ophthalmoscope, and he put a stethoscope to their chests. After these cursory examinations, he asked Mrs. Santana if the boys had a lot of friends. She said that they did. He asked her if they gave her any bad trouble around the house, and she said that they didn't. The doctor took out a piece of paper and wrote, "Vicente and Emilio Santana were seen by me today for apparent behavioral disorder. There is no physical explanation for their emotional behavior. I advise that they be referred for psychological evaluation if they are unable to function acceptably at school." He handed the note to Mrs. Santana, who handed it to Vicente and told the boys to go back to school with it. The boys were never referred for psychological evaluation, and that was the last Mrs. Santana heard of the matter.

Walking home alone at one o'clock, Mrs. Santana felt irritated that she had missed her favorite noontime *novela*. She was also upset by the trouble the boys had caused her. Life would have been easier if she hadn't had Vicente Santana's children to worry about, she thought. Several years ago, when one of Mrs. Santana's caseworkers found her similarly beset with worries about one or another of her children's school suspensions, he had asked her why she had had nine children. He had been sure she had not had them simply to get more welfare. Anyone who had spent five years as a caseworker, as he had, knew that life for Puerto Rican women like Mrs. Santana was far more a series of accidents, both happy and unhappy, than popular wisdom would have it. It was not in Mrs. Santana's nature to think about what she was going to eat for dinner until an hour or so before dinnertime, and it was not in her nature to go to bed with a man thinking that it might lead to an increase in her welfare check. Still, even the caseworker was surprised by the way she had laughed at his question. Why had she had nine children? Surely the answer was obvious. *"Los tenía porque los tenía,"* she had said ("I had them because I had them").

When Carmen Vásquez married Rafael Rodríguez, at the age of fourteen, she knew nothing about birth control. Four children came of that relationship: the boy who had died; Casilda; Rafael, Jr.; and Felipe. When she took up with Angel Castillo and became pregnant, before she was living with him and before her marriage to Rafael Rodríguez had come to an end, she decided to have an abortion. The abortion was performed by a midwife, who charged her fifty dollars and caused her a great deal of physical pain. While she was lying on the midwife's kitchen table, half in shock, certain that she was about to die, her late mother appeared to her as if in a vision. The mother reminded her daughter that she had died having an abortion, and urged her never to have another one. The vision unsettled Carmen, and she vowed that she would heed her mother's advice. Shortly after the abortion, she became pregnant with Hilda Castillo. Nine months after Hilda was born, Inocencia was conceived. After Inocencia's birth, Carmen wanted to get her tubes tied, but she thought — rightly or wrongly — that in Puerto Rico a tubal ligation required a husband's consent. Angel Castillo liked children. (He is now thirty-eight and has had thirteen children by five women.) When Carmen asked his permission to have a tubal ligation, he refused to give it.

In New York, Mrs. Santana learned about birth control. Before she could put her newly acquired knowledge into practice, she became pregnant with Vicente Santana. After Vicente's birth, she tried taking birth control pills. The pills caused her to miss her periods, so she stopped taking them. Emilio was born nine months after she took her last pill. After Emilio's birth, Mrs. Santana attempted to use a diaphragm, with a conspicuous lack of success: Gabriel was a diaphragm baby. Mrs. Santana had intended to get a tubal ligation after Gabriel's birth, but his illness and subsequent hospitalization interfered with her plans. By the time the three-month-old Gabriel was home from the hospital, Mrs. Santana was pregnant with María. She had a tubal ligation before leaving the hospital with María. The days when Mrs. Santana felt her life would have been easier if she had not had her last four children were balanced by the days when she felt it was a shame that she had had her tubes tied, because it would have been nice to have a baby with Delgado. Mrs. Santana likes babies. When her thirteen-year-old daughter Inocencia's first child was born and she feared that Inocencia wouldn't be able to care for him, she offered to take on the task of raising him.

Shortly after Mrs. Santana got home from the clinic, Casilda telephoned. After Casilda had given her mother a précis of the *novela* episode she had missed, she asked why Vicente and Emilio had been suspended. "Oh, it was nothing, they were just laughing," Mrs. Santana said. It was Casilda's cue to chide her mother again for not taking life seriously enough. Casilda wished her mother would punish her children when they were suspended, instead of making light of their suspensions. In retrospect, Casilda was almost grateful for her stepmother's strict upbringing. She felt it would enable her to do a better job of raising her children than her mother had done. She was critical of her mother for having let Felipe drop out of the Work Incentive Program, for letting María and Vicente suck their thumbs, for condoning Vicente's sleeping with girls. She prided herself on keeping a tidier house than her mother and on being a better disciplinarian. Helen Figueroa's schoolteachers were not convinced that Casilda was much of a disciplinarian. Felipe had dropped out of Work Incentive at sixteen, Helen Figueroa had dropped out of a Head Start Program at five. At nine, Helen sucked her thumb, drank from a bottle, wet her bed, and often missed school. That morning Casilda had overslept ten minutes and had not sent Helen to school. She said to her mother on the phone, "The teacher marks Helen absent if she gets there ten minutes late, so what's the point of sending her?"

Mrs. Santana has never been to the Empire State Building, to Radio City Music Hall, or to any of New York City's other tourist attractions. She has never seen a play or a circus, visited a museum, or belonged to a social or political organization. She goes back to Cayey for a week every two or three years, but she has never been to Queens ("I don't know anybody over there"), and she hasn't been to midtown Manhattan in years. Although Mrs. Santana's life is limited geographically and culturally — she spends most of her time with her family and friends in Brooklyn and on the lower East Side — it is filled with exciting events. A brief account of some of the events that she was a party to in the weeks after Emilio's and Vicente's suspensions from school would include these items:

Jesús returns to Casilda after an absence of two weeks. Casilda forgives him again for his transgressions. Casilda and Jesús have a party on a Saturday evening. During the party, Mrs. Santana's bronchitis bothers her, and she goes to the bathroom to take her medicine. She spends fifteen minutes in the bathroom. When she rejoins Delgado, who is high on Scotch and marijuana, he accuses her of having spent the time on the street flirting with men. A loud quarrel ensues. Mrs. Santana yells over the *merengue* playing on the stereo that she was barely able to climb the four flights of steps to Casilda's apartment once, and could not possibly have done it twice in one evening. Casilda's apartment is ideally suited to dancing: the stereo is the only piece of furniture left in the living room. A week ago, Casilda sold the living room set she and Jesús had bought for eight hundred dollars in 1974 — and had not quite finished paying for — for seventy-five dollars. The furniture was still in fair condition, but Casilda hoped to get Jesús to prove his devotion to her by putting a down payment on a new set of furniture. She didn't think he would buy new furniture until there was nothing left to sit down on in the living room.

•

Delgado's cousin's husband dies accidentally of an overdose of pills that were prescribed for his nerves. Mrs. Santana takes her four youngest children to see the body. For weeks afterward, Gabriel has nightmares and insists on sleeping with the light on in the bedroom.

•

Helen Figueroa doesn't return from school one afternoon. Casilda calls her mother to ask if Helen is at her house — she isn't — and then goes out to look for her at the homes of several friends. By seven o'clock, Casilda hasn't found Helen. She becomes convinced that Helen has been kidnaped, and calls the police. Casilda and the police find Helen in a classmate's apartment at midnight, sound asleep. The police get angry with Casilda when she wakes Helen and hugs her instead of spanking her. "How can I spank her when I'm just so glad to find her?" Casilda asks.

•

Jesús stays away from Casilda's still bare apartment for another week. When he comes back, Casilda throws him out. The next day, Alfonso Ortiz moves in. Alfonso finds a shabby sofa and two threadbare easy chairs on the street and carries them up to the apartment. Jesús spends a week with

Aida González, who then leaves him and returns to her husband. Jesús goes to Connecticut to visit his father, loses his job, returns to New York, gets another job, and moves in with Mrs. Santana. He pays her fifteen dollars a week for his food and the use of the living room sofa.

•

Gabriel's teacher sends Mrs. Santana a note. The note says, "Gabriel acted in a very dangerous manner on Thursday. He picked up chairs and threw them at another boy in his class. He cursed me and then ran out of the room. He is in danger of being suspended from this school if he does not learn to control his temper. Please sign this note and have Gabriel return it to me." Mrs. Santana reads the note and puts it in her pocketbook, where she keeps most of her other important papers — Delgado's paycheck stubs, her rent receipts, her letters from the employment specialists — but she does not sign it. Gabriel had told her about the episode before the note came. He had thrown the chairs at the boy because the boy had cursed Mrs. Santana three times, he said, and he couldn't let him get away with that. Mrs. Santana agreed. She said she didn't bother the teachers with her children's conduct at home and she was fed up with the teachers' complaining about their behavior at school. She does not receive a second note from the teacher. Gabriel is not suspended.

•

Mrs. Santana gets around to taking María to the ophthalmologist, who prescribes glasses for her. The ophthalmologist decides he might as well examine Mrs. Santana's eyes, too. He discovers she has a growth on one eye, and removes the growth a few days later. Mrs. Santana's eye is red and sore for a week. For a week or so, María enjoys the novelty of wearing glasses. Then she stops wearing them and loses them.

•

At a party at Mrs. Santana's one evening, Jesús meets Juanita Gómez, one of Mrs. Santana's upstairs neighbors. He dances with her. Juanita's husband gets jealous because Jesús is holding her close, and starts a fight with Jesús. A few days later, Juanita and her husband part. Jesús moves in with Juanita and her three children. A week later, he breaks up with Juanita and returns to Mrs. Santana's living room sofa.

•

A heroin addict is murdered a block from Mrs. Santana's apartment.

•

Casilda is tired of supporting Alfonso with her welfare check and wants him to get a job. "When I tell you to go to work, you act as if I'd cursed your mother!" she screams at him one morning. Casilda and Alfonso have a fight. Alfonso throws Casilda's piggy bank out the window. Casilda takes her children and goes to her mother's house. Her mother and the four Santana children rejoice: they do not care much for Alfonso and hope she will take Jesús back. Casilda doesn't see any point in living with Jesús again, but she wishes she would hear from her family and friends that he was talking about her more; she feels he owes her at least that much after their six years together. Alfonso goes to Brooklyn in the evening. He and Casilda make up. Casilda whispers to her mother that her marriage to Alfonso will not last long and that she wishes she weren't with him. Casilda and Alfonso return to the lower East Side.

•

Georgina and a black man who Mrs. Santana says is Georgina's pimp steal a wallet. The police come up to Georgina and Felipe's apartment before they have a chance to dispose of the wallet. Felipe agrees to take the rap. He spends a night in jail, is charged with a misdemeanor, and receives a suspended sentence.

•

Casilda, who sold numbers before her son was born in 1972, starts selling numbers again. She earns several hundred dollars in two weeks, makes a down payment on a new set of living room furniture, and spends most of the rest of the money on clothes for herself and the children. Her spirits improve with her affluence.

•

Emilio goes to the lower East Side after school one day and doesn't return home. At midnight, Mrs. Santana calls the police to help her look for him. They find him at a friend's house. Mrs. Santana wallops Emilio, to the satisfaction of the police.

•

Georgina's eight-year-old son, who is fifty pounds overweight — he suffers from a glandular condition — goes to the hospital to have an operation. He claims that a nurse hit him and says he doesn't like the hospital food. Georgina takes him out of the hospital before he can be operated on.

•

Margie Mendoza's husband dies on the sidewalk near Mrs. Santana's apartment building, of complications resulting from chronic alcoholism, a day after Mrs. Santana has dreamed that he would die on the street.

•

Casilda discovers that she is pregnant, and has an abortion. After the abortion, she gets an I.U.D.

•

Georgina learns that she is pregnant. She keeps meaning to have an abortion but doesn't get around to it.

•

Isidro Colón, the man who got Roberto Figueroa into the heroin business, accuses Roberto of fooling around with his wife. Isidro shoots Roberto in the chest at point-blank range. Roberto is taken to Bellevue Hospital to have a bullet removed from his lung. Isidro flees to Puerto Rico. The police ask Roberto Figueroa who shot him; he says he doesn't know. Shortly after Roberto is released from Bellevue, he has a fight with his wife. Another man intervenes to stop Roberto from beating her. Roberto shoots him. Roberto flees to Puerto Rico. Rafael Rodríguez, Jr., assumes Roberto's position in the heroin business. He takes Alfonso into the business, and, against his better judgment, his own brother Felipe.

O N a Saturday evening several weeks after Rafael Rodríguez, Jr., had advanced from selling heroin on the streets of the lower East Side to having others sell heroin for him, Casilda and Alfonso gave a party. Seventy or eighty men, women, and children, including Rafael, Mrs. Santana, her four youngest children, and Francisco Delgado, went to the party. Since the occasion for the party was Jesús Manrique, Jr.,'s birthday, his father had been invited. Jesús and Alfonso spent the evening exchanging wary glances. Rafael's companion that evening was Diana López, from Dover. Rafael had spent the previous week with Rosa Cruz. One afternoon, he had told Rosa he was going to the Bronx to see a friend. Instead of going to the Bronx, he had driven to Dover to see Diana. He had returned with Diana to her mother's apartment on the lower East Side.

The atmosphere inside Casilda's apartment was festive. In the darkened living room and in two of Casilda's three small bedrooms, well-dressed couples danced to very loud music, holding each other tight. At midnight, when the party was still getting underway, the birthday candles were lit and Jesús, Jr., cut his cake. Casilda's Instamatic camera recorded the ceremony for the family photo album. The children ate ice cream and cake, and drank some of the grownups' beer and liquor whenever the grownups' backs were turned. Some of the children got drunk, not to anyone's surprise or disapproval. A pot of *sancocho,* a Puerto Rican stew, bubbled on the kitchen stove. The only room where there was no dancing was Casilda's bedroom. Mrs. Santana sat on Casilda's double bed next to the youngest guest at the party, a sleeping one-month-old baby. Delgado sat on a nearby chair, drinking Scotch neat, paper cupful after paper cupful. Mrs. Santana was wearing a bouffant black wig that Casilda had given her and a new pair of purple slacks and a matching print blouse. She didn't feel like dancing — her mind was on a trip she wanted to take to Puerto Rico — and anyway Rafael had given her a brown paper bag filled with money to hold for him, as well as a small box that had once contained nails and now contained heroin.

On Friday morning, Rafael had bought an ounce of pale brown Chinese heroin from his connection for eighteen hundred dollars. On Friday evening at Diana's mother's apartment, Rafael had cut the ounce of heroin with two ounces of milk sugar. Then Diana had helped him divide the whitened mixture into a thousand decks. (A deck is the amount of adulterated heroin that fits into the neck of a tube of toothpaste.) Later, Diana's mother had wrapped each deck in cellophane. Rafael had sold some of the decks of heroin to Alfonso, to his brother Felipe, and to his other salesmen for six dollars a deck. The salesmen would resell them on the street for ten dollars a deck. Rafael had already made about ten thousand dollars dealing in heroin. He had spent most of the money on Rosa's and Diana's apartments, on a trip to Puerto Rico with Diana, and on a wardrobe of flashy clothes. That Saturday evening, Rafael, a wiry, soft-spoken, intense young man of twenty-four, was wearing a red blazer and a pair of white satin slacks. Rafael had posted three armed guards on the landing outside Casilda's fifth-floor apartment. The guards scrutinized every person who came up the stairs. Despite these precautions, Rafael appeared tired and overwrought. He seemed to be enjoying neither the deference now being accorded him as a heroin dealer nor his new prosperity. The tension that came from dealing in heroin and from sustaining relationships with two women was proving hard on him.

Rafael had been a ladies' man since his early teens. He had cared no more for his harsh stepmother than Casilda had, but whereas she remembers feeling like a woebegone Cinder-

ella, Rafael looks back on his youth as a series of romances
with young women. "In Cayey, my first girl was Catherine," he says. "Catherine was supposed to be my engage-
ment girl. I didn't touch anything except her lips. Debby
was my weekend girl. I had one child with her. Then there
was Mabel. My father kept telling me to go to school, but
instead I'd take off with Mabel for the cemetery." Late in
1968, Rafael dropped out of the eleventh grade in Cayey and
came to New York, where he was glad to be with his mother
and Casilda, and where he found another series of women.
"There was Judy, who lost her virginity in my mother's
apartment," he says. "I shared her with my brother Felipe.
She had a child and we didn't know whose it was. Then I
had Paz. She was recently killed by her husband. Then
Ana. She was in her thirties and lived in my mother's building. Ana had ten kids and was on welfare. When I couldn't
get along with Vicente Santana anymore, I moved out of my
mother's apartment and moved in with Ana. I got her pregnant. She was too possessive, and I soon got tired of her.
When I couldn't figure out a way to get away from her, I
joined the Army."

Rafael, who was nearly twenty, went through his ten weeks
of basic training at Fort Jackson, South Carolina, in the fall
of 1970 and was then shipped to Fort Ord, in Monterey, California, for several months of advanced infantry training. He
learned from a clerk that his whole platoon was scheduled to
be sent to Vietnam. To avoid having to go to Vietnam —
"I didn't feel like going so far away," he says — he applied
for the paratroopers. He was sent to Fort Benning, Georgia.
"First they had to push me out of the plane, then I got to like
jumping," he recalls. In the spring of 1971, Rafael went

to New York on a five-day pass. His intention was to visit Rosa Cruz, a lethargic classmate of his sister Inocencia Castillo, but while he was in New York he saw Diana López, whom he had known in Cayey when she was a little girl. Diana was then fifteen, and he fell in love with her. He stayed on in New York with Diana when his five-day leave was over, and got a job in a hat factory, using a friend's Social Security number. In March of 1972, the Army caught up with Rafael. He had dodged his pursuers many times, and suspects he was finally turned in by his former girl friend Judy. By then, he was tired of hiding. He was taken to the Brooklyn Navy Yard to be photographed and fingerprinted, and from there to Fort Dix, New Jersey, where he was beaten and locked up in a dark cell for three weeks. He was asked if he wanted to go back to the Army. "Before I went AWOL, I had already decided to re-enlist," Rafael says. "I loved the Army. I didn't have anything besides the Army. I was far away from trouble, and I loved the traveling. But after I was caught I felt I wasn't going to be comfortable in the Army anymore, so I got out. Diana had just had my child and I hadn't yet given my daughter my name, and that was on my mind."

Rafael, dividing his time between Diana and Rosa, spent most of 1972 in Dover, where he worked in a factory for three dollars and sixty-nine cents an hour, and in New York, where he found odd jobs. Late in 1972, he went to Puerto Rico with Diana and quickly worked his way up from the kitchen of a tourist hotel in San Juan to waiting on tables, to tending bar. Diana was jealous because Rafael was writing to Rosa, and she left Puerto Rico for Dover early in 1973. In the spring of 1973, Rafael returned to New York to be with

Rosa. That summer, Diana and Rosa had several fist fights before agreeing to share Rafael. In the fall of 1973, Rafael was taken into the heroin business by Roberto Figueroa, Casilda's first husband, who was also Diana's nephew.

The noisy, merry party at Casilda's place was interrupted at about three in the morning by one of Rafael's sentries, who burst into the living room to announce that Rosa's apartment had been robbed. Rafael left abruptly with his guards. Returning an hour later, Rafael told his mother that thieves had broken into Rosa's apartment. They had taken eight hundred dollars in cash, a stereo tape deck worth seven hundred dollars, and two television sets. Rafael said he was glad Rosa had not been there during the burglary because she might have been hurt. Late as it was, Rafael called in several of his salesmen and started selling them heroin; he wanted to make good Rosa's losses by the next day.

Two weeks after Casilda's party, Mrs. Santana made up her mind to go to Cayey to visit her two daughters Inocencia and Hilda Castillo and some of her other relatives. She went to a travel agent in her neighborhood and booked two round-trip tickets to Puerto Rico — one for herself and one for Gabriel. On her last trip to Puerto Rico, in 1972, Mrs. Santana had taken María along; this time it was Gabriel's turn. The tickets were for the night flight of the following welfare-check day. On check-day morning, Mrs. Santana waited more anxiously than usual for the mailman; if her check failed to arrive, she would have to postpone her trip. Her check did arrive, and she went straight to the travel agency to buy the tickets. Her check covered all but a few dollars of the two fares. Casilda had given her mother enough money from her numbers earnings to pay the rent; Delgado had given her eighty dollars to spend in Puerto Rico; she was going to let the bodega and furniture store bills ride.

Mrs. Santana and Gabriel flew to San Juan on a jumbo jet, waited an hour at the Puerto Rico International Airport at San Juan, and boarded a small plane for the short flight over the mountains to Ponce. They landed in Ponce at five in the morning. Inocencia Castillo and her husband, Reynaldo Figueroa, were at the airport to meet them. Inocencia is a plump, vivacious girl of seventeen, with long black hair (her father's "good" hair), a pretty face, and bad teeth, which she longs to have improved with gold. Reynaldo is thirty-two. While Reynaldo drove his truck to Cayey, across green and brown countryside, Gabriel dozed and Mrs. Santana and Inocencia chattered incessantly. They reached Inocencia and Reynaldo's house just as the local roosters were crowing.

Reynaldo and Inocencia live in a ramshackle wooden house — one of a cluster of ramshackle houses huddled together along a road a couple of miles outside Cayey. The main part of the house consists of three small bedrooms, a small living room, and an ample kitchen. The rooms are separated by flimsy partitions, and lack doors; the floors are concrete; the roof is tin; and the furniture looks very old. There is a shower in a large, separate, roofless room in back of the house, and a toilet in another large, separate, roofless room out back. The toilet is broken. Inocencia and Reynaldo live in the house with their two children — Eduardo, who is three, and Tina, who is only a few months old — and with Reynaldo's nine-year-old daughter by his previous mar-

riage. The woman Reynaldo married in 1965 in the double
ceremony with Casilda and his brother Roberto refuses to
give Reynaldo a divorce.

When Reynaldo's truck pulled into the dirt front yard, an
old man who stank of rum and urine and who worked for
Reynaldo to earn rum money, was slowly turning a roast pig
on a large stick over a fire. Reynaldo earns his living as his
parents had once done: he raises pigs, butchers them, cooks
them, and sells the meat. Mrs. Santana took off her new red
pants suit. She asked Gabriel to take off her fashionable, un-
comfortable platform shoes, which she couldn't unlace. She
lay down on Inocencia and Reynaldo's lumpy mattress,
where Tina was sleeping, told the sleeping baby she was fat
and beautiful, and went to sleep. When she woke up, she
took an outdoor shower and changed into a pair of Bermuda
shorts she had fished out of her suitcase. She sent Gabriel to
a bodega about thirty feet away for some bread, soda, and
lunch meat, and settled down on a vinyl and wrought-iron
chair in Inocencia's small living room to visit with her
daughter. The day passed quietly. People came by on foot
and in cars to buy small amounts of roast pork. They
pointed to the part of the pig they wanted. Reynaldo cut the
meat and weighed it on a small scale and wrapped it for them
in plain brown paper. A truck filled with oranges pulled up
alongside the houses, and Reynaldo bought a sack of a
hundred oranges for two dollars. Reynaldo's daughter
played with a dozen neighborhood children in the garbage-
strewn back yard and in a vacant lot across the road, where a
few goats grazed and some chickens scrabbled. Eduardo had
no toys and got into constant mischief. Inocencia's way of
handling him was similar to Casilda's way of rearing Jesús

Manrique, Jr.: she alternately shouted at him, hugged him, spanked him, and asked him for kisses.

In the late afternoon, Mrs. Santana took out of her pocketbook the gold earrings María had been given by her godmother and told Inocencia to wear them until María was old enough to wear them herself. If the earrings were safely installed in Inocencia's pierced ears, Georgina wouldn't be able to get her hands on them again. Mrs. Santana also gave Inocencia a small gold charm, which Francisco Delgado had sent to Tina. Inocencia had chosen Delgado to be Tina's godfather — an honor she would never have accorded her previous stepfather, Vicente Santana, whom she blamed for causing her to leave her mother's house. Santana had first attempted to seduce Inocencia when she was eleven. Inocencia had complained to her mother, who had advised her to sleep with a baseball bat beside her bed. After that incident, Inocencia thought she might be better off living with her father in Cayey, and went there. She missed her mother and returned to New York at the end of six months. When she came back, Santana tried to get into bed with her. She slapped him in the face. Shortly afterward, she went to bed with an eighteen-year-old man whom she had met on the lower East Side. She fancied she loved him, and wanted to marry him. For some reason unknown to Inocencia, the young man's mother didn't approve of her and broke up the romance. Inocencia felt that, being no longer a virgin, she would be too vulnerable to Santana under his roof, and went to live for a while with Casilda and Jesús. Casilda was afraid that Inocencia would start fooling around with Jesús — or vice versa — so Inocencia went to live with Rafael and Ana. In the summer of 1971, when she was thirteen, she met Reynaldo Figueroa, who was twenty-seven. Reynaldo got her pregnant and then abandoned her to return to his wife in Cayey. Inocencia dropped out of the seventh grade. She went back to her mother, who had by then moved to Brooklyn with Delgado. Two months after Eduardo's birth, Reynaldo appeared and took Inocencia and Eduardo away to his parents' house in Dover. Mrs. Santana had been very angry with Reynaldo for deserting Inocencia during her pregnancy. She wasn't sure if Inocencia had gone willingly to New Jersey or had been abducted, so she had set off by bus for Dover with Delgado and Diana. In Dover, Inocencia told her mother that she was content with Reynaldo and wanted to stay with him. Reynaldo didn't like the cold weather; early in 1973, he and Inocencia returned to Cayey. Inocencia's moods are variable. Sometimes, after an hour of feeding and diapering and reprimanding the children, she tells her mother she is going crazy in her terrible house in Cayey. She says that if she can't get a decent house she will fly off to New York with her two small children. Sometimes, when the children are napping, she says she is happy with Reynaldo and thinks she will stay with him for the rest of her life. "If I can," she says.

At five in the afternoon of that first day in Cayey, Mrs. Santana watched a bus drive up and let out a couple of dozen sugarcane workers — they earn about a dollar-fifty per hour — and then asked Reynaldo to drive her into town. When she comes to Cayey, she always stays with her favorite *tía* — her mother's youngest sister, who had built a house on the site of her grandparents' house, where she was born and raised. *Tía's* house is a warren of small rooms on a hillside eight or ten blocks from the center of town. It is more sub-

stantial than Inocencia's house, has indoor plumbing that occasionally works, and is more peaceful. *Tía* lives with her
husband, her youngest son, his wife, and their newborn
baby. She is sixty-five and looks ten years older. *Tía* gave
up her own bed for Mrs. Santana. Gabriel slept on a cot.
Mrs. Santana gave her *tía* twenty-five dollars for their food
and lodging. *Tía's* husband, an invalid, had long been accustomed to sleeping on the living room sofa. One evening
when Mrs. Santana and her *tía* were watching television in
the living room while *tía's* husband slept, Mrs. Santana
laughingly recalled that her grandfather had also been put on
the living room sofa during his old age — he drank a lot of
rum and was no longer of any use in bed.

On Mrs. Santana's second day in Cayey, she walked from
tía's house to the house of Angel Castillo's mother, her
former antagonist, where Hilda lives. When Mrs. Santana
saw Hilda, she greeted her as casually as if it had been only a
few days since they had last seen each other, instead of more
than two years. Hilda's features are almost as pretty as Inocencia's, but she had dyed her shoulder-length hair red and
had curled it in an unbecoming way. She wore clothes that
looked uncomfortably tight, and she appeared aloof. Inocencia attributed her sister's standoffishness to the fact that she
was so well educated. Hilda had just finished high school,
and was about to go to secretarial school. Mrs. Santana was
glad that Hilda had stayed in Puerto Rico. She approved of
Hilda's studies — she often said that she wished María
would "stay in school and not marry young" — but, not
having raised Hilda, she seemed to have a greater affection
for Inocencia, whose life had followed the pattern of her
own. During her week in Cayey, she spent three days at

Inocencia's house and saw Hilda only four times; their visits never lasted more than fifteen minutes, and their conversation was impersonal. Mrs. Santana didn't ask Hilda whether she had a boy friend, and Hilda's attitude toward her mother was notably cool, in sharp contrast to the attitude of the rest of Mrs. Santana's children.

While Mrs. Santana was in Cayey, she spent a day visiting half a dozen other relatives, including the *tía* with whom she had stayed after her brother Jaime Ramírez's wife made her feel so unwelcome in her apartment in New York in 1959. If there was a highlight of her week, it was her meeting with Angel Castillo, her favorite husband. She couldn't go to his house to see him — his wife would not have permitted that — so she contrived to see him late one evening at the house of a friend, after her *tía* and Gabriel had gone to bed. Mrs. Santana and Angel had a few beers and some laughs for old times' sake. Neither of them felt inclined to make love. Before they said goodbye, Angel Castillo gave her twenty dollars.

On the next-to-last day of her stay, Mrs. Santana came down with a severe attack of bronchitis. She had contemplated spending her last two days in Puerto Rico visiting her father and another of her mother's sisters in San Juan; instead, she stayed in bed. When she got on the plane for New York, she said she hoped she would win the latest New York State Lottery. If she won, she would have enough money to build a house in Cayey, and only if she owned a house could she afford to live there. Gabriel cried on the plane home. He had loved Puerto Rico — the warm, clean air, the peaceful streets — and he had wanted very much to stay there.

WHEN Mrs. Santana returned from her trip to Puerto Rico, at three in the morning, she was greeted by an assortment of bad news. Vicente and Emilio had broken a windowpane in their bedroom; the landlord would not be pleased. The boys had also played hooky for five straight days, and a truant officer had come around to look for them. Francisco Delgado had skipped two days of work; Mrs. Santana didn't know how she would be able to catch up on her bodega bill. Worst of all, Rafael Rodríguez, Jr., had become curious enough about the product he was dealing in so lucratively to sample it. The needle he had used in trying his first shot of heroin had given him a serious infection. He had been taken to Bellevue Hospital, and had been told he would have to spend six weeks there. Before going off to Bellevue, Rafael had entrusted his cash to Felipe, who had squandered it. Felipe had also borrowed some money from Casilda to buy heroin; he had squandered that, too. The money Casilda had lent Felipe was the cash she had to have on hand to pay off her customers if they bet on a winning number. She didn't dare risk selling numbers without it, so she had been obliged to stop selling numbers. Casilda was broke again and felt understandably dispirited.

Even the mail that had come during Mrs. Santana's absence meant possible trouble; there were two letters from the Department of Social Services. One of them was a "notice of intent to reduce public assistance due to receipt of duplicate check." According to the department's records, Mrs. Santana had claimed that her May 16, 1974, check for two hundred seventy-two dollars hadn't arrived. A replacement check had been issued to her on May 22, 1974. Now the department claimed that Mrs. Santana had fraudulently cashed both checks, and intended to retrieve its overpayment in twelve semimonthly installments of twenty-two dollars and sixty-six cents. She hadn't cashed both checks — she suspected that the original check had been stolen and that someone had forged her signature on it — but she envisioned half a dozen trips to her local welfare center to straighten the matter out. The second letter began:

DEAR SIR/MADAM,

New York State regulations require that your eligibility for a public assistance grant be re-established periodically.

Your case has been selected by the Division of Eligibility Control to receive a complete investigation by our Face to Face Recertification Program.

You must appear for your scheduled interview on . . .

You are required to bring with you proof of your continued eligibility for public assistance on the above date and time. A list of documents you must bring to the interview is attached . . .

Failure to keep an appointment and/or submit necessary documents will result in the closing of your case . . .

The list of necessary documents included "proof of school attendance" for anyone on the case "between the ages of 6 and 21." Mrs. Santana would have to obtain a false report card or a letter from school or a current bus or train pass or a current lunch pass for Inocencia if she wanted to keep her on the case.

The day after her night flight from Puerto Rico, Mrs. Santana slept late. When she got up, in midafternoon, María and Lillian were in the living room watching a television show. On the screen, a six-year-old child was reading a book. María watched, marveling at the child's ability, and said to her illiterate friend, "Lillian, you ought to go to school and learn to read and write like that kid. That way, when you grow up and get married and your husband goes to jail, you'll be able to write him a letter."

Mrs. Santana cooked some rice and beans, diced salt pork, and bananas. She left most of the food on the stove for Delgado and the children; with a plateful of food in a brown paper bag, she set off for Bellevue to visit Rafael. She made the trip by gypsy cab to avoid climbing up and down subway stairs. It took her twenty minutes to make her way through Bellevue's grimy corridors to the ward where Rafael lay; a plastic tube was dripping antibiotics in a glucose solution into a vein in his arm. A week in the hospital had done Rafael a lot of good. He had put on some weight. His eyes were clear. He looked rested and somewhat at peace with himself. Diana was with him when Mrs. Santana arrived. Rosa had gone to visit Rafael his first day in the hospital, had run into Diana there, and had told Rafael that she wouldn't come to see him anymore if he allowed Diana to visit him, too. Rafael had told Rosa that it wouldn't be right to keep Diana away; the result was that Rosa had dropped out of his life for the time being.

When Mrs. Santana approached Rafael's bed, she didn't rebuke him for having sampled heroin. Nor did Rafael apologize for the folly of having done so. Rafael told his mother that he had learned his lesson: when he got out of the hospital, he wouldn't try heroin again. He would go back to selling heroin "for a very short while," just to make some money; then he would get a regular job in a factory, marry

Diana, and settle down. Mrs. Santana didn't believe that Rafael's plans would ever be realized. It was far more likely, she feared, that he would go back to selling drugs and would get caught; she worried that Rosa would turn him in to the cops, as Judy had turned him in to the Army. Nevertheless, Mrs. Santana nodded, as she always did when her children told her of their plans — as she had nodded when Casilda told her she would get Helen through high school and when Felipe, spaced out as usual, had said, "I'm going to make something of myself, just wait and see."

Mrs. Santana has never given much thought to the future. The present requires all the attention she can muster. Casilda recently asked her if she was going to marry Francisco Delgado. "No," she said. "There's no point in doing that. I've told you, I don't have good luck with men." Casilda went on to ask her mother whether she thought she would always live with Delgado. It has been a long time since Mrs. Santana thought that marriages last forever, and after a while she gave the best answer she could: "You never can tell."

A day or so later, she and Delgado quarreled, and Delgado spent the night on the living room sofa. In the morning, she told him that if he was planning to leave her he should leave now, while she was still young and could find another man.

"So that's what you want — for me to leave you," Delgado said.

"Not today," she said.

Afterword

MANY OF THE LETTERS I received after the Profile of Carmen Santana was published in *The New Yorker* contained questions about how I had carried out the reporting for the piece. Some of the questions were easy to answer. *Q*. Do you speak Spanish? *A*. Yes, thank heavens; I have adequate Spanish. *Q*. Is Mrs. Santana a composite character or an actual person? *A*. An actual person. I changed her name, birth date, and a few other minor details in order to protect her from probable Department of Social Services repercussions. Some of the questions required longer answers. How had I found Mrs. Santana? How much time had I spent with her?

How had I won her trust? How much of my information was obtained firsthand? (Excerpt from a typical letter: "How did you know when Mr. Delgado went to bed 'with his clothes on,' when the children went to bed, and when Mrs. Santana went to bed? Did you accompany Mrs. Santana to the school principal's office, to Bellevue Hospital, to Puerto Rico?") A number of readers suggested that I follow up the Profile by writing a Department of Amplification on what a sociologist-reader called my "methodology and technology" and what a less sociologically oriented reader called my "bag of tricks." I like the idea of possessing tricks and, such as they are, I am happy to let them out of the bag here.

When William Shawn, the editor of *The New Yorker,* approved my idea of writing a Profile of a Puerto Rican welfare mother, in early January 1973, I assumed I would find a subject within a week; there were, after all, tens of thousands of Puerto Rican welfare mothers in New York City. Despite a network of helpful friends, my search for a subject took almost three months. I first called an old friend in the mayor's office, who introduced me to the mayor's policy assistant on such matters as welfare, who in turn referred me to a woman employed by a health clinic on the lower East Side. This woman referred me to several of her coworkers at the health clinic. The tenth or twelfth coworker was sympathetic to the story I had in mind to write and set up an interview for me with a Puerto Rican welfare mother of her acquaintance. The interview was a disaster. The woman was extremely suspicious of me, answered my questions in monosyllables when she answered them at all, and looked at her watch every five minutes. After two hours, she said she had to leave. I asked if I might return another day. She shook her head emphatically and told me it would not be necessary: she had already told me all she knew. I gathered she had reluctantly consented to my visit to oblige her acquaintance at the health clinic. She didn't particularly trust her and she would never trust me. I confess to having assumed that one or another of New York City's tens of thousands of Puerto Rican welfare mothers would trust me; after half a dozen time-consuming and dispiriting false starts I came to see that this assumption was a rash one.

I went to see friends, and friends of friends, who were settlement house directors in Puerto Rican neighborhoods, Puerto Rican politicians, and priests with parishes in various Puerto Rican sections of the city. I learned that these settlement house directors, priests, and politicians were not close enough to their constituencies or flocks to be able to persuade any member of them to confide in me, although several of them were kind enough to try — a useful lesson, but one that didn't bring me closer to a subject. By early March, it was even more obvious to me than it had been previously why so many magazine articles were written about politicians, movie stars, sports figures, and other publicity seekers: had I begun a "Profile" of, say, a U.S. senator or an NFL quarterback in early January, it would already have been completed.

I think I kept looking for a Puerto Rican welfare mother partly because I have a personal aversion to writing about people who employ press secretaries or public relations representatives, that is, people who want to be written about; partly because I had a deep interest in Puerto Ricans, as a result of having read and admired Oscar Lewis's books and of having done a couple of "Talk of the Town" stories for *The New Yorker* on the city's Puerto Rican subculture; and

also — a reporter's pride! — because the prospect of having
to tell William Shawn that I couldn't find a single Puerto
Rican welfare mother to talk to in all of New York was simply too embarrassing.

My luck improved in mid-March. A friend's husband,
who was about to resign from the Department of Social Services and move out West, suggested I phone one of his col-
leagues, a caseworker I shall call Louis Steiner. In March
1973, Louis Steiner was spending most of his time at a desk
in a welfare center in Manhattan, but from 1965 until 1971,
before the caseworker system changed, he had made count-
less home visits to welfare clients on the lower East Side.
When we met for coffee and he talked about some of the
Puerto Rican welfare mothers he had known, I found him extremely knowledgeable about them and sympathetic toward
them. Louis Steiner immediately understood what I wanted
to do. Unfortunately, he didn't quite approve of my plans.
He thought it would be better for me to write a piece about
several welfare mothers rather than a "Profile" of a single
welfare mother, and he kept saying so. I spent the next week
meeting Louis Steiner in coffee shops, delicatessens, bars,
and Chinese restaurants, trying to convince him that there
was as much truth implicit in the facts about one person as
there was in the facts about a dozen people. By writing
about many welfare mothers I would, perhaps, have more
facts but no more truth, and I would lose the vividness, the
felt truth one gets only when writing about a single person. I
quoted a favorite English professor of mine to Louis: "A
great figure in art is both singular and representative, which
is why we keep going to see *Hamlet*." Perhaps to avoid any
future discussions of either Shakespeare or truth, Louis fi-

nally agreed to help me. He briefly described several of the
Puerto Rican welfare mothers he thought might be willing
subjects. The first one to whom he proposed to introduce me
backed out at the last minute. The second was Carmen Santana.

Louis and I made an appointment to see Mrs. Santana on
the afternoon of March 23, 1973. Mrs. Santana was clearly
happy to see Louis and she seemed happy to see me. As she
later told me, Louis had been nice to her when he was her
caseworker and, although she saw him infrequently since her
move to Brooklyn, her daughter Casilda still found him helpful when she went to her local welfare center, where he
worked. Louis told Mrs. Santana that I was a writer and
wanted to write the story of her life. She nodded noncha-
lantly, as if she were accustomed to meeting such writers
every day of the week. I liked her at once and enjoyed the
lively domestic scene that swirled around her. I took a few
notes. My note-taking didn't bother Mrs. Santana, but it
may have been a good thing that she couldn't decipher my
Speedwriting. I had scrawled a few first impressions, for example, "men's clothes hanging on pegs in her bedroom."
(Many months later, I asked Mrs. Santana whether she had
believed Louis when he had told her I was a writer that first
afternoon. "No," she said. I asked her what she had
thought I was, expecting to hear that she had me tagged as a
new subspecies of welfare employee. "Louis's girl friend,"
she replied, laughing heartily.) As Louis and I were leaving,
I made an appointment to see Mrs. Santana on my own one
morning the following week.

I found Mrs. Santana at home alone when I showed up at
eleven o'clock the following Wednesday. Again, she

seemed happy enough to see me. I believe in beginning at beginnings, so I asked her about her grandparents, her parents, and her childhood in Puerto Rico, which she seemed content to discuss. It is a writer's good fortune that most people enjoy talking about themselves, especially those who rarely have an occasion to do so. After a while, Mrs. Santana began to steal glances at her watch — an unnerving reminder of my first attempt at interviewing a Puerto Rican welfare mother — but it turned out that she only wanted to be sure to see the noon installment of her favorite *novela* on TV. It seemed to give her pleasure to brief me on the many characters who were lying, cheating, embracing, haranguing, and whispering their way through its complicated plot. After one o'clock, we talked some more about her early years in Puerto Rico. When the children came home from school, they also made me feel welcome. By three-fifteen, I was longing for a cup of coffee, and gave the children money to go out and buy a paper carton of coffee for me and some soda for themselves. I left a little later, after making another morning appointment to see Mrs. Santana.

I decided that Mrs. Santana wouldn't take it amiss if I brought the makings of lunch for the two of us, so I arrived for our second interview with a loaf of French bread, some butter, and assorted cold cuts. I was very glad I had. Although Mrs. Santana is not much of a coffee drinker herself, she had seen how grateful I had been for the coffee on my previous visit and had bought half a pound of Bustelo coffee and a quart of fresh milk especially for me. She set about making it as soon as I walked in. Louis Steiner had been Mrs. Santana's caseworker at the height of her difficulties with Vicente Santana. On this visit, I asked her to tell me about him, which she did with apparent glee. We again watched the noontime *novela* and then looked at the snapshots in her family photo album.

Our fourth or fifth meeting happened to occur on a check day in April. I asked Mrs. Santana how much her check was for. She showed it to me. I asked her if she could manage on what I took to be the grant for five people — herself and her four youngest children. She told me she was receiving the grant for seven people; her daughter Inocencia and Inocencia's first child had lived with her briefly in 1972 and had been legally on her case, but had returned to Puerto Rico some months earlier. She hadn't had them taken off her case, she said, and asked me if I thought she should. One of the occupational hazards of being a reporter is affecting by one's mere presence the events one is there only to record. I said it was none of my business. I think Mrs. Santana trusted me pretty well from the outset — she withheld a fact or two at first, but hers is a trusting nature and her trust was not so much won as freely given; I know that when several more weeks went by and the grant for seven kept coming, she decided she could tell me anything without suffering adverse consequences. One day in late May, as I was inquiring how she budgeted the grant for seven, she told me about Francisco Delgado and his financial contribution to her household. Each time I went to see Mrs. Santana, I had left her apartment by four o'clock: for one thing, she hadn't yet volunteered to tell me about the owner of those men's clothes on the bedroom pegs; for another, I figured it was safer for me to make my way past the dope dealers and junkies in her neighborhood in broad daylight. That afternoon, she invited me to stay for dinner. I tried to decline. "What's the mat-

ter, Susan, you got something against pigs' ears? My
mother's a terrific cook,'' Gabriel said. That was no invita-
tion, that was a challenge, and it had to be accepted. I
stayed.

When Francisco Delgado came home from work at five
o'clock, it was obvious that he knew who I was. He, too,
was friendly, and didn't appear threatened by my knowledge
of his domestic arrangements. When dinner was over, Emilio offered to walk me the few blocks from the apartment to
the approach to the Williamsburg bridge, where cabs were
easy to find. He intuitively knew I would feel safer walking
with him than walking alone. After several more months
went by, however, I got to know so many people in Mrs.
Santana's neighborhood that I felt they wouldn't let anyone
harm me, which gave me the freedom to stay at Mrs. Santana's apartment as late as necessary. I would not have written that Francisco Delgado went to bed with his clothes on at
one o'clock, or when the children and Mrs. Santana went to
bed, had I not been there to see the family turn in. Virtually
all of the information in the Profile was obtained at firsthand.

This is perhaps the place to answer more fully the question
so many *New Yorker* readers put to me: wasn't I often in fear
of my safety while researching the Profile? As I have just
acknowledged, at the outset that was sometimes the case.
The first time I climbed the steps to Casilda's first-floor apartment to interview her, I encountered three junkies in the process of shooting up on the third-floor landing. Like the
young boy who whistled as he walked alone through the
woods, I smiled at them and said I hoped Casilda was home
because there were too many stairs to climb for nothing.
They nodded and let me by. Soon I was a familiar figure on

Casilda's block, too, and moved about without fear, taking only a few precautions, such as traveling by cab rather than subway when I stayed with her until 4:00 A.M. To my surprise, there were always a welcome number of cabs looking for fares in that neighborhood at that hour of the morning. While I was researching the Profile, it often occurred to me that it was an advantage, from the point of view of safety as well as from other points of view, to be a woman. Francisco Delgado would probably not have cared to have Mrs. Santana spend so much of her time alone with another man. Non–Puerto Rican women seem less threatening to the residents of a Puerto Rican neighborhood than non–Puerto Rican men. I was particularly aware of this when I brought my husband, Neil, to the party of Casilda's described in the Profile. Neil could easily be taken for an Irish detective. He would never have been safe going up those stairs alone. I walked ahead of him to tell the three sentries Rafael had posted outside Casilda's apartment that he was my husband and was okay. Inside the apartment, of course, neither of us was in danger from the other guests, but when Mrs. Santana, who had been holding Rafael's heroin, got up to dance and handed the heroin to me, I prayed that the New York police would not be dropping by. It is a commentary on the problems of a reporter in our time that I wound up being much more afraid of the legal authorities, who have taken to sending reporters to jail for refusing to reveal their sources, than I had ever been of Mrs. Santana and her friends and relatives.

After going to see Mrs. Santana once or twice a week for five or six months, I knew her a great deal longer and better than I had ever come to know most people I'd written about in the past. Still, I felt that a "Profile" of Mrs. Santana would benefit from being researched over an even longer period, and I was fortunate to be able to arrange my schedule so that I could write several more conventional articles while continuing to see Mrs. Santana and her family.

Additional time was needed because there were so many people in the family and in the neighborhood (Mrs. Santana's doctor, her numbers man, her Italian friend, Margie Mendoza) to talk to. Some people — Rafael, for example, who was shuttling between Diana, in Dover, and Rosa, in Brooklyn, and getting started in the heroin trade — were too preoccupied to see me in the fall of 1973. Rafael was much easier to interview when he was in Bellevue Hospital for six weeks, recovering from the infection the heroin needle had given him in 1974. The sequence of melodramatic incidents that occurred long after my first six months with Mrs. Santana also gave me — and, I hope, the reader — a better understanding of the quality of her life. The slow process of going over a single event with many people, and going over it every few months with one person, was also useful. As the months passed, Mrs. Santana and her children learned that four-letter words didn't bother me any more than pigs' ears; they gradually stopped using their Sunday-best language and stopped withholding details they thought might offend my non–Puerto Rican sensibilities. The account I got from Mrs. Santana of Mr. Santana's marital infidelities in late 1974 was far more entertaining and bawdy than the account I got from her in the spring of 1973. Best of all, the passing of time enabled me to go from being a question-asking, note-taking stranger to being a friend of the family. Although I usually keep my family life and my working life separate, I became so interested in Mrs. Santana that I not only brought Neil with me to visit her but often brought our two young daughters. Soon there was no need for a notebook, and while the young Santanas and the young Sheehans rummaged together for buried treasure in the back yard rubble, I could fade quietly into the background. After a year I felt I enjoyed the invisibility of that happily placed creature reporters so rightly envy: the fly on the wall. What was overheard, or seen out of the corner of an eye, often proved as valuable as what was asked directly — if not more so.

Mrs. Santana was an ideal Profile subject for many reasons. Unlike U.S. senators or NFL quarterbacks, she had a great deal of free time, which my visits helped to fill. If I didn't call her for a few weeks, she would call me to see how I was. She liked me to accompany her on her errands, often making me feel my presence helped give her the strength she required to face a school principal or an employment specialist. When Mrs. Santana suddenly decided to go to Puerto Rico, she asked me to come along so that I could see for myself how pretty her home town was, and how handsome her favorite husband was. I flew to Puerto Rico with Mrs. Santana, Gabriel, and one of our daughters. Mrs. Santana's *tía* shared a room with the four of us. *Tía* slept in a single bed, the children slept in sleeping bags, and Mrs. Santana and I occupied a double bed.

Among Mrs. Santana's other virtues was honesty. In the summer of 1973, I asked two of Louis Steiner's friends who worked in the welfare center in Brooklyn, where Mrs. Santana's case record was stored, to lend me her file. When, unbeknown to her, I read it, I learned that everything she had told me that was capable of being confirmed by the written record was, indeed, confirmed by it. A final virtue: Mrs.

Santana never regarded any of my questions as an invasion of her privacy. On the contrary, she always led me to believe that she preferred my most outrageous personal questions — those about her love life, for instance — to my questions about her ancestors, who held so little interest for her.

When the Profile was published, I had known Mrs. Santana for two and a half years. If there was a trick in my bag, the trick was time.

One of the first telephone calls I received after the article appeared was from Louis Steiner. He asked the question so many readers were later to ask: what did Mrs. Santana think of the Profile? I told Louis she hadn't read it and probably never would. Even if I had used real names in the Profile, it would have been rather too long for her taste. With all the names of the people and places and the specific birth dates changed, she would have found it hopelessly confusing. Most subjects do read the articles one writes about them, and one tends, as one writes, to concern oneself with their reactions. Knowing that Mrs. Santana wouldn't read the Profile gave me the freedom to write about her exactly as I wanted to, without having to worry about causing her pain. Louis knew that Mrs. Santana had been introducing me to her friends as *"la escritora que escribe la historia de mi vida"* ("the writer who is writing the story of my life"). Didn't I think she would be disappointed if I never produced the story? "No," I said, with conviction. So few of the plans Mrs. Santana made were ever carried out that she would scarcely expect me to write something simply because I had set out to write it.

Numerous readers were curious to know what had happened to Mrs. Santana after the Profile appeared. A few asked, "Where will it all end?" The most significant event in Mrs. Santana's life in the last year has been the death of her son Felipe Rodríguez. One day, Felipe quarreled with Georgina and came to stay for a while with Mrs. Santana. She found him in bed one morning, dead of an overdose of heroin. I had known and she had known (though she might not have admitted it) that Felipe was doomed, but his death came even sooner than I had expected. As for where it will end, it is not easy to foresee Casilda's daughter finishing high school and getting a decent job. It is, alas, far more likely that Helen will drop out of school, get pregnant at an early age, and become the third generation of Mrs. Santana's family on welfare.

Rock Valley College

DEMCO